PASTA
EVERY WAY FOR EVERY DAY

PASTA
EVERY WAY FOR EVERY DAY
Eric Treuillé & Anna Del Conte

PHOTOGRAPHY BY IAN O'LEARY

DK

DK Publishing

LONDON, NEW YORK, MELBOURNE,
MUNICH, and DELHI

US TEAM
SENIOR EDITOR
Barbara Berger
RECIPE CONSULTANTS
Wesley Martin
Barbara Bowman, Gourmetsleuth
EDITORIAL CONSULTANT
Jane Perlmutter
DTP DESIGNER
Milos Orlovic

UK TEAM
MANAGING EDITOR
Stephanie Farrow
DTP DESIGNER
Sonia Charbonnier
EDITORIAL CONSULTANT
Rosie Kindersley
DESIGN AND ART DIRECTION
Stuart Jackman
PROJECT EDITOR
Julia Pemberton Hellums
EDITORS
Sally Somers and Anna Brandenburger
PRODUCTION CONTROLLER
Elizabeth Cherry
FOOD STYLING
Eric Treuillé

Second American Edition 2004
2 4 6 8 10 9 7 5 3 1

Published in the United States by
DK Publishing Inc.,
375 Hudson Street, New York, New York 10014

DK Publishing, Inc. offers special discounts for bulk
purchases for sales promotions or premiums. Specific, large-
quantity needs can be met with special editions, including
personalized covers, excerpts of existing guides, and
corporate imprints. For more information, contact:
Special Markets Department,
DK Publishing, Inc.,
375 Hudson Street, New York, NY 10014
Fax: 212-689-5254

Cataloging-in-Publication Data
is available from the Library of Congress

ISBN 0-7566-0368-4

Color reproduction in Italy by GRB
Printed and bound by L.Rex Printing Company Ltd, China

Discover more at
www.dk.com

CONTENTS

Introduction **6**
Notes from the Cooks **7**

THE PASTA
The Ten Commandments **8**
The Tools—Pasta in the Kitchen **10**
The Tools—Pasta at the Table **12**
Which Pasta? **14**
Which Sauce? **15**
Long Pasta—Strands and Ribbons **16**
Short Pasta—Tubes and Shapes **18**
How Much Pasta? **20**
The Salt **21**
The Boil **22**
The Bite **23**
The Drain **24**
The Toss **25**

THE RECIPES
PASTA WITH TOMATOES **28**
PASTA WITH BUTTER AND CHEESE **44**

PASTA WITH MUSHROOMS **54**
PASTA WITH SEAFOOD **62**
PASTA WITH MEAT **78**
PASTA WITH OLIVES AND OLIVE OIL **96**
PASTA WITH GREENS AND HERBS **102**
PASTA WITH BEANS AND LENTILS **120**
PASTA WITH GARLIC **126**
PASTA WITH PEPPERS AND EGGPLANT **132**
FRESH AND FILLED PASTA **142**

Think Ahead Tips **148**
Pasta in the Pantry **150**
Pasta Planner **152**
Pasta on the Menu **154**
The Chop—Size Guide **156**
The Skills—Top Tips **158**
Notes from the Cooks on Ingredients **160**
Index **162**
Mail Order Sources **167**
How We Make Our Books **168**

INTRODUCTION

The Italians, who are masters at combining sophistication with simplicity, have eaten pasta for the past millennium or so. They know that no other food can nourish and delight so easily, while asking for so small an effort on the part of the cook. Simple yet sustaining, a dish of pasta satisfies our hunger yet invites the eye and pleases the palate with its countless shapes, colors, and flavors. It is the most versatile of foods, changing its character with ease, according to season, occasion, cook's mood, or time available.

In this book we concentrate mainly on dried pasta, which is the pasta that the Italians eat religiously and lovingly every day of every week. It is the pasta they always have on hand, and it is the pasta that pairs most successfully with the greatest number of different sauces.

Some of the sauces we have chosen are classic, others are modern, and many are variations on a traditional theme. There are slow-simmered sauces that can be prepared totally ahead of time, as well as many quick-fix sauces that can be made just before eating, so a whole meal can be put together in half an hour or less. Put together, yes, but always with love, care, and attention. When the family is nearly ready to eat, the pasta is slid into a pan full of boiling water and the cook shouts *Ho messo giù la pasta* — I've put the

pasta in. A few minutes later everyone sits down in silence and the cook brings in the bowl of steaming pasta and sets it in the middle of the table for people to serve themselves. Pasta is a convivial, sharing food; to our mind, it is best not formally plated.

We leave the last word to the actor Alberto Sordi in the wonderful movie *A Taxi Driver in America:*

Dove c'è pasta, c'è speranza

Where there's pasta, there's hope.

Anna Enic

NOTES FROM THE COOKS

BEFORE YOU COOK read through the recipe carefully. Make sure you have all the equipment and ingredients required.

ON COOKING TIMES

Always take cooking times as guideline rather than gospel. In each recipe, we qualify estimated cooking times with a description of how the ingredient should look at the end of cooking time, for instance "cook until soft, 5 minutes." It is better to cook the ingredient until its appearance matches the given description rather than simply setting the timer.

Various factors affect cooking times, with your choice of pan and the character of your oven at the top of the list.

The size and shape of a pan directly affect how quickly a dish will cook. The same sauce cooked over the same heat will cook faster in a wide, shallow skillet and more slowly in a tall, deep pot. The larger cooking surface of a wide skillet ensures rapid evaporation, while the high sides of deep pots actually inhibit evaporation. In each recipe, we have specified the size and shape of pan required for a quick cooking or slow cooking sauce.

Ovens vary from kitchen to kitchen. Most have hot spots, so be prepared to rotate dishes from top to bottom or from front to back during cooking time. An oven thermometer is a useful kitchen tool, allowing you to match your oven's temperature with the one specified in the recipe. Always allow a margin of 5–10 minutes either way for baking times.

ON TASTING

Always taste food as you cook and before you serve. Don't be afraid to add or change flavors to suit your palate—the fun of cooking is in experimenting, improvising, creating. Ingredients differ from day to day, season to season, and kitchen to kitchen. Be prepared to adjust sweetness, sharpness, spiciness, and, most important of all, salt, to your own taste.

ON SALT AND PEPPER

Discerning seasoning makes the difference between good and great food. As a general rule, seasoning is best done toward the end of cooking. The optimum moment for a cook to judge how much salt and pepper a recipe requires is at the end of cooking time, when the flavors have blended.

ON MEASURING

Accurate measurements are essential if you want the same good results each time you follow a recipe.

A good set of measuring cups is the most accurate way to measure dry ingredients.

We recommend using cooks' measuring spoons when following a recipe. All spoon measurements in the book are level unless otherwise stated. To measure dry ingredients with a spoon, scoop the ingredient lightly from the storage container, then level the surface with the edge of a straight-bladed knife.

We use standard level spoon measurements:
 1 tablespoon = ½ fluid ounce
 1 teaspoon = ⅙ fluid ounce

To measure liquids, choose a transparent glass or plastic measuring cup. Always place the cup on a flat surface and check for accuracy at eye level when pouring in a liquid to measure.

A final and important rule of measuring—never measure ingredients over the mixing bowl!

THE TEN COMMANDMENTS

Pasta is everyday food, yet any Italian knows that the cooking and serving of it calls for care and attention. Remember these ten golden rules for perfectly cooked pasta every time.

- Buy good quality Italian pasta.

- Use a large pot full of water.

- Salt the water with a generous hand.

- Boil the water and keep it boiling.

- Stir the pasta often—it will stick if you don't!

- Start timing when the water returns to the boil.

- Don't wander off! As they say in Italy, *gli spaghetti amano la compagnia*—spaghetti loves company.

- Drain immediately, but not too thoroughly.

- Have the sauce and a warmed bowl ready.

- Eat up! The only time people stop talking in Italy is when a bowl of pasta is placed on the table.

PASTA IN THE KITCHEN

The key to making perfect pasta is to start with the right pot. When cooking 1lb dried pasta, the pot should hold about 5 quarts of water to give the pasta plenty of room to move around.

A pot made of an inexpensive, lightweight metal like aluminum is ideal, since it conducts heat evenly and is easy to lift when full of boiling water. A stockpot will also make a good pasta pot, as it is usually taller than it is wide and has two sturdy handles for lifting.

A large colander is also essential. A colander has the advantage over a strainer in that the water drains more slowly, which will prevent the cooked pasta from becoming a sticky mass. Choose a colander with feet so that the base stands well above the cooking water when it is emptied into the kitchen sink.

The type of pan used to cook a pasta sauce will directly affect the required cooking time and character of the

finished sauce. The larger cooking surface of a wide skillet ensures rapid evaporation, which is essential for a quick cook sauce.

A heavy-bottomed, deep pot is best for a slow cooked sauce. The high sides guard against overevaporation and the heavy bottom prevents sticking when a long simmering time is required.

1. Tall, narrow, lightweight pasta pot with a lid
2. Long handled wooden spoon for stirring pasta
3. Large colander with feet
4. Large skillet for quick-cook sauces
5. Heavy-bottomed pot with a lid for slow-cook sauces

PASTA AT THE TABLE

In an Italian home, pasta is always served from a large bowl set in the middle of the table. A wide bowl with shallow sloping sides is traditional. If the bowl is too deep the high sides will inhibit the tossing, and therefore the proper saucing, of the pasta. As soon as the pasta and its sauce are together, they must be tossed immediately. A large fork and spoon, or two forks, do the job best.

Pasta is a simple food. The success of a pasta dish will owe much to the quality of its ingredients. In Italy, freshly ground black pepper and freshly grated cheese are basic necessities, making a cheese grater and a pepper grinder essential equipment, both in the kitchen and at the table.

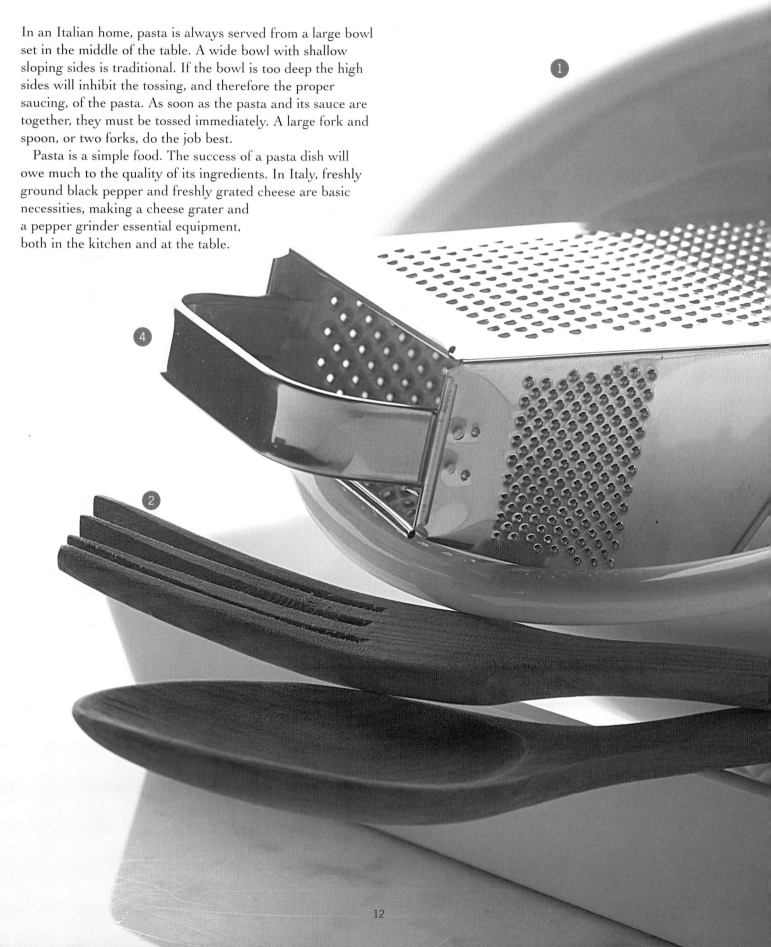

1 Large bowl for tossing and serving
2 Large fork and spoon for tossing
3 Pepper grinder
4 Cheese grater
5 Ovenproof baking dish

WHICH PASTA?

WHAT IS GOOD PASTA?

There is only one important rule to remember when buying pasta. Good ingredients are essential for good pasta.

• Choose pasta made from one hundred percent durum wheat. Always check that the package reads either *pasta di semola di grano duro* or "durum wheat pasta." Durum wheat is a hard wheat grain—in fact the hardest wheat grown. Pasta made with durum wheat will maintain its shape, texture, and flavor while cooking in rapidly boiling water.

• Choose pasta made in Italy wherever possible. In Italy, both the composition and the manufacture of dried pasta are tightly controlled by law. Pasta produced in other countries can be made from ordinary soft wheat flours or from blends with durum wheat. When cooked, pasta made from inferior types of flour will have a limp, sometimes gluey, texture as well as a tendency to overcook.

PLAIN OR EGG?

Dried pasta divides into two types: pale yellow plain pasta made with durum wheat and water, and golden yellow egg pasta made with durum wheat and whole eggs. Egg pasta has a smoother, silkier texture; plain pasta has a firm, chewy bite. Neither is superior to the other—they are simply different. In Italy, it is the sauce that determines the choice between dried plain pasta and dried egg pasta. Oil-based sauces are usually served with plain pasta and butter-based and cream-based sauces with egg pasta.

FRESH OR DRY?

We still come across the widespread misconception that fresh is better. This is not so. Truly fresh pasta that is worth buying is made with good quality flour and real eggs and no other additives. Finding this can present a challenge. We will always choose a quality boxed dried pasta imported from Italy over a prepackaged fresh pasta from the supermarket.

Homemade fresh egg pasta is another story. The finest fresh pasta is always made at home, using the best ingredients. Turn to pages 144–145 if you have the time and the enthusiasm to learn how.

WHICH SAUCE?

There are said to be six hundred different pasta shapes in Italy. Of these, about fifty are the common shapes that are easily found. But, since different regions of Italy and different manufacturers sometimes give different names to the same shape, there is often confusion. So, when pairing pasta with sauce, it is best not to focus on all the different shapes of pasta. Think instead about the pasta sauce—its consistency and texture—and which pasta it would coat and complement best. As a general rule, slippery or more delicate sauces are best paired with long pasta strands or ribbons. Short pasta shapes and tubes suit thicker or chunkier sauces that cling to the hollows of the pasta and get caught inside the holes. But remember, cooking and eating pasta is no different from all cooking and eating; whatever venerable traditions and classical rules there may be, always trust your own palate. At the end of the day, it's a matter of personal choice.

LONG PASTA - STRANDS & RIBBONS

Long and thin dried pasta ribbons and strands should be dressed with light, oil-based sauces which allow the strands to remain separate and slippery. Strands and ribbons that are thicker, such as bucatini or tagliatelle, are best when paired with sauces based on cream, cheese, and eggs, or with sauces based on meat. Dried egg pasta ribbons, such as fettuccine and pappardelle, also pair well with these same types of sauces. A good guideline for matching long pasta to sauce is whether the sauce ingredients will cling to the pasta when it is twirled on a fork.

1. Pappardelle - *Broad egg ribbons*
2. Tagliolini - *Very thin egg ribbons*
3. Fettuccine - *Thin egg ribbons*
4. Tagliatelle - *Medium egg ribbons*
5. Bucatini - *Thick hollow strands*
6. Linguine - *"Little Tongues" - Thin ribbons*
7. Spaghettini - *"Little Spaghetti"*
8. Spaghetti - *Thin strands*
9. Capellini - *"Fine Hair" - Very fine strands*

SHORT PASTA - TUBES & SHAPES

When matching short pasta to sauce, be sure that the size of the pasta complements the size of the sauce ingredients. The chunkier the ingredients in the sauce, the larger the hollow or cup required to capture them. This is an important guideline to follow in order to allow a balanced mouthful of sauce and pasta to be enjoyed when the finished dish is eaten. Pasta tubes and shells come in many different sizes. Large pasta tubes and shells are excellent paired with rich meat sauces, robust vegetable sauces, or used in baked dishes. Medium-sized short pasta tubes, shells, or shapes go well with vegetable sauces and are also good for pasta salads.

1 Orecchiette - *"Little Ears" - Medium disk-shaped shells*

2 Conchiglie - *"Conch Shells" - Shell-shaped pasta, available in different sizes*

3 Gnocchetti - *"Little Dumplings" - Ridged, shell-shaped pasta*

4 Chifferi - *Elbow-shaped tubes, available ridged and smooth*

5 Penne - *"Quills" - Diagonally cut tubes, available smooth or ridged and in different sizes*

6 Rigatoni - *Large ridged tubes*

HOW MUCH PASTA?

There is no rigid rule about how much pasta to cook. It all depends on whom you are feeding and what else you are feeding them. A traditional meal in Italy has no "main" course, it is rather a succession of harmonious courses of which pasta is usually one. Outside Italy, pasta is generally served as the main event, making a complete meal when paired with a crusty loaf of bread and a fresh green salad. A good rule of thumb is to allow about ⅛lb for a first course serving and ¼lb for a main course serving. The recipes in this book will generally serve about 6 people as a first course and 4 people as a main course.

THE SALT

The addition of salt to the pasta cooking water is an essential step that must not be omitted. When pasta is cooked in unsalted water no matter how flavorful the sauce, the dressed pasta will be certain to have a bland taste.

• Use a coarse grain or flaked salt with no additives. Coarse or flaked salt will dissolve more quickly than a fine grain salt.
• We always use coarse grain sea salt or kosher salt. The quality of salt does matter, since different salts have different flavors and levels of saltiness.
• Add salt to the boiling water 1–2 minutes before the pasta to give the salt time to dissolve.
• When cooking 1lb dried pasta, add about 1½ tbsp kosher salt to 3–4 quarts of boiling water.

THE OIL MYTH

If you use the correct amount of water, add the pasta when the water is boiling rapidly, and remember to stir the pasta immediately, the addition of olive oil becomes totally unnecessary. It is in fact a waste of olive oil.

THE BOIL

WHEN TO ADD IT ?

When the water is salted and boiling, slide in the pasta all at once. All the pasta must be added at the same time to ensure that it cooks uniformly.

Stir immediately with a long wooden fork or spoon to prevent the pasta from sticking to the bottom of the pot. During cooking, stir occasionally to keep the pasta in constant motion.

HOW LONG TO COOK IT ?

Always start timing from the moment the water returns to a rapid, rolling boil after the pasta has been added to the pot. The actual cooking time will depend on the quality, size, and shape of the pasta. Use the timings printed on the package only as a guide. The way to know when the pasta is cooked is to take some out and take a bite. We advise you to begin testing about 2 minutes before the package instructions suggest it should be done.

THE BITE

IS IT DONE ?

As with all cooking and eating, the ideal point of doneness is always a matter of personal taste. As a general rule, pasta is perfectly cooked when it is tender but still retains some resistance—meaning you should still feel its texture when you bite into it.

Al dente literally translates as "to the tooth," but "to the bite" is probably a more useful description.

UNDERCOOKED ?

The pasta will still have a chalky core and a slight taste of raw flour.

OVERCOOKED ?

The pasta will have lost all its springy and chewy qualities.

COOKING FRESH PASTA

Uncooked fresh pasta is heavier because it contains more moisture than dried. Allow about ¼ lb for a first course serving, ⅓ lb for a main course serving.

Don't skimp on the cooking water. The right proportion of water to pasta is even more critical in the case of fresh.

Fresh pasta cooks in very little time, so make sure that the sauce is ready and the bowl warm before you slide the pasta into the water. Once the water returns to a boil, begin testing for doneness after 1 minute.

THE DRAIN

When the pasta is done, it must be drained immediately. Every second the pasta remains in the hot water it will continue to cook.

• Be ready. Have your colander in the sink. As soon as the pasta is firm to the bite, tip it from the pot into the colander and give the colander two or three sharp shakes.

• Don't overdrain. Draining pasta properly is important. Pasta should never be overdrained. It should remain slippery so that it can be properly coated with the sauce. How well drained the pasta should be depends on the type of pasta and its shape.

• Long pasta strands or ribbons should be left still lightly dripping with water.

• Short pasta tubes or shapes should be drained more thoroughly since their hollows and holes will hold more water.

• Fresh egg pasta needs the least thorough draining. It should remain very slippery with water after draining since it tends to absorb more of the sauce than a plain dried pasta.

• Don't rinse pasta or add oil to it. Rinsing pasta causes it to lose the stickiness needed to help the sauce cling. Adding oil will, likewise, keep the sauce from sticking to the pasta.

BEFORE YOU DRAIN

When the recipe specifies, we suggest that you remove about half a cup of the pasta water from the pot and set it aside just before draining. Use the reserved water to adjust the consistency of the finished dish when it is needed. If the pasta is overdrained, if the sauce is too thick, or if the sauced pasta is too dry, add a few tablespoons of the reserved pasta water. Using the pasta water is always preferred to adding hot water from the tap since the cooking water contains the pasta starch and salt. This adds both body and seasoning as well as moisture to the finished pasta dish.

THE TOSS

Speed is essential when saucing, tossing, and serving pasta. Have everything you need on hand. Make sure your family or guests are gathered at the table and ready to eat.

• Don't delay! Sauce the pasta as soon as it has been drained. Pasta should never be allowed to sit in the colander without any sauce. Always have the sauce hot, ready, and waiting.

• Sauce the pasta in a warmed serving bowl or in the still-warm pasta cooking pot. Even better is to add the pasta straight to the sauce in the skillet. Tossing everything together in the skillet in which the sauce was cooked provides a warm surface to ensure the pasta blends perfectly with the sauce.

• Use two large forks, or a large fork and a spoon, to toss the pasta. Mix well, until every strand or piece of pasta is lightly and evenly coated with the sauce. If the pasta seems dry, drizzle in a little of the reserved pasta cooking water (see page 24). The starch in the water helps the sauce to cling to the pasta and to coat every surface as uniformly as possible.

• Don't oversauce. The sauce should moisten, not drown, the pasta. It is not only the sauce that gives flavor to a pasta dish. The pasta has a taste and character of its own. You want the taste of the pasta as well as the sauce to come through.

• Pasta cools quickly, so have warmed serving dishes ready. Place an ovenproof serving bowl or individual dishes in a 250°F oven to warm through while you cook the pasta. Or, just before serving, place in the sink and pour hot water over bowl or dishes.

CHEESE

Always use fresh Italian Parmesan and always grate it freshly just before using. Grated Parmesan, however, is not an essential accompaniment to each and every pasta dish. In Italy, it is certainly never added indiscriminately. Parmesan is traditionally associated with richer and creamier sauces. Its addition would be considered heresy in many shellfish dishes, and it is even considered an optional extra on many olive oil-based vegetable and tomato sauces.

The Recipes

PASTA WITH TOMATOES

TOMATOES IN THE PASTA PANTRY

Canned tomatoes are an essential pantry basic to be kept on hand at all times. Always choose canned tomatoes over unripe and out of season fresh tomatoes—even if it means changing your menu accordingly. There's no need to discard any leftover canned tomatoes not required in the recipe; canned tomatoes in their juice refrigerate and freeze well. A quick and easy way to chop up whole canned tomatoes is to use kitchen scissors to chop them while they are still in the can. When making a slow-simmered tomato sauce, you can add the tomatoes whole from the can and break them up in the pan with a wooden spoon.

Tomato paste is best bought in a tube since it keeps well in the refrigerator and can be used a spoonful at a time. If you have opened a can, you can freeze any leftover tomato paste not required in the recipe. Simply freeze the remaining paste in the can and, when it has frozen solid, open the base of the can with a can opener and push out the block of paste. You can then cut it into slices, put it back in the freezer, and use each slice as needed.

Although jars of sun-dried tomatoes in oil are a handy pantry item, packaged sun-dried tomatoes have a superior flavor. Seek them out in gourmet stores and from mail order sources (see page 167). If buying loose, make sure they are still chewy and not too dry. To soak, place in a bowl with 1tbsp red wine vinegar, pour boiling water over to cover, and let stand until tender and swollen.

Choose fresh tomatoes that are firm, red, and at their seasonal best. Plum tomatoes are the ideal variety for pasta sauces because their flesh is thick and meaty. When flavor is a priority, however, ripeness is more important than variety. When cooking with fresh tomatoes outside their peak season, it's well worth thinking ahead and buying the tomatoes a few days in advance of using. Set them on a tray by the kitchen window, making sure they are not touching, and leave for a few days to ripen. Never store tomatoes in the refrigerator; chilling gives the tomato flesh a mealy texture.

Taking the extra time and care to peel fresh tomatoes will make for a finished dish with a superior texture, flavor, and appearance. However, when time is at a premium, it is a step that can be skipped. See page 156 for how to peel and seed fresh tomatoes.

NO COOK
RED PESTO

SERVES 4
½ cup sun-dried tomatoes in oil,
 drained
2 garlic cloves, crushed
2½ tbsp pine nuts, toasted
½ tsp crushed red pepper flakes
5 tbsp extra virgin olive oil
½–2 tsp balsamic vinegar
black pepper
1lb dried pasta

Place tomatoes, garlic, pine nuts, red
pepper flakes, oil, and vinegar in a food
processor; pulse to a smooth paste. Add
vinegar and pepper to taste. Set aside
or store, see below. Cook pasta in a
large pot of boiling, salted water, until
firm to the bite if serving hot, or just
firm to the bite if serving as a salad.
Drain, reserving ½ cup pasta water. Return
pasta with pesto to the warm pasta pot.
Toss well to coat, adding reserved water
as needed. Serve immediately or at
room temperature.

WHICH PASTA?
Strands or shapes—spaghettini, spaghetti, penne.

THINK AHEAD
Make pesto up to 4 days in advance. Cover and
refrigerate. If serving as a salad, dress pasta up to 8
hours ahead. Cover and store at room temperature.

VARIATIONS
RED PESTO WITH ARUGULA
Add 2 handfuls arugula leaves with the
pesto and the drained pasta to the warm
pasta pot. Toss and finish as directed.

RED PESTO WITH BASIL
Add 1 handful torn fresh basil with the
pesto and the drained pasta to the warm
pasta pot. Toss and finish as directed.

NO COOK
FRESH TOMATO

SERVES 4

1lb dried pasta
6–7 medium-sized ripe tomatoes, seeded and diced
1 garlic clove, crushed
5 tbsp extra virgin olive oil
salt, black pepper

Cook pasta in a large pot of boiling, salted water, until firm to the bite if serving hot or just firm to the bite if serving as a salad. While pasta is cooking, combine tomatoes, garlic, and oil. Add salt and pepper to taste. Let stand while pasta is cooking to allow the flavors to blend. Drain pasta. Toss drained pasta with marinated tomatoes in a large serving bowl. Serve warm or at room temperature.

WHICH PASTA?
Strands or thin ribbons—spaghetti, linguine.

THINK AHEAD
Make sauce up to 8 hours in advance. Cover and store at room temperature. If serving as a salad, dress pasta up to 8 hours in advance. Cover and store at room temperature.

VARIATIONS
FRESH TOMATO AND MOZZARELLA
Return drained pasta with tomatoes and 2 cups diced mozzarella to warm pasta pot. Toss well to coat. Serve immediately.

FRESH TOMATO AND LEMON
Add 1 tbsp fresh lemon juice and ½ tsp grated lemon zest to the tomatoes. Finish as directed.

FRESH TOMATO, RED ONION, AND BASIL
Add ½ finely sliced red onion and 1 handful torn fresh basil to the tomatoes. Finish as directed.

FRESH TOMATO AND OLIVES
Add 10 sliced pitted black olives, such as kalamata or gaeta, to the tomatoes. Finish as directed.

FRESH TOMATO, ARUGULA, AND BALSAMIC VINEGAR
Add 2 tsp balsamic vinegar and 1 handful roughly chopped arugula to the tomatoes, garlic, and olive oil. Finish as directed.

NO COOK
SUN-DRIED TOMATO WITH CHILI, GARLIC, AND BLACK OLIVES

SERVES 4

1lb dried pasta
12 sun-dried tomatoes in olive oil, drained and sliced
1 cup pitted black olives, such as kalamata or gaeta, sliced
3 garlic cloves, finely chopped
½ tsp crushed red pepper flakes
1 tsp red wine vinegar
6 tbsp extra virgin olive oil
1 tbsp chopped fresh basil or flat-leaf parsley
salt, black pepper

Cook pasta in a large pot of boiling, salted water, until firm to the bite if serving hot. Slightly undercook the pasta if serving this dish as a salad. While pasta is cooking, combine tomatoes, olives, garlic, red pepper flakes, vinegar, and oil. Drain pasta. Return pasta with basil or parsley and tomato mixture to the warm pasta pot. Toss well to coat. Add salt and pepper to taste. Serve immediately or at room temperature.

WHICH PASTA?
Strands or thin ribbons—spaghetti, linguine.

THINK AHEAD
Mix sauce ingredients up to 8 hours in advance. Cover and store at room temperature. If serving as a salad, dress pasta up to 8 hours in advance. Cover and store at room temperature.

QUICK COOK
PUTTANESCA
SERVES 4

1lb dried pasta
5 tbsp extra virgin olive oil
½ tsp crushed red
  pepper flakes
2 garlic cloves, finely sliced
6 anchovy fillets, drained
  and chopped

2 - 14oz cans Italian
  plum tomatoes, chopped,
  or 2lbs fresh
  tomatoes, chopped
1¼ cups pitted black olives,
  such as kalamata or gaeta
1 tbsp capers, drained
salt, black pepper

Cook pasta in a large pot of boiling, salted water, until firm to the bite. While pasta is cooking, heat oil in a skillet. Add red pepper flakes, garlic, and anchovies. Cook, stirring constantly over medium heat, until anchovies have disintegrated, 2–3 minutes. Raise heat to medium high, add tomatoes, and cook, stirring occasionally, until thickened, 15 minutes. Add olives and capers. Add salt and pepper to taste. Drain pasta. Add pasta to the hot sauce. Toss well to coat. Serve immediately.

WHICH PASTA?
Strands or tubes—spaghetti, penne, rigatoni.

THINK AHEAD
Make sauce up to 3 days in advance. Cover and refrigerate.

COOKS' NOTE
The name derives from *puttana*—prostitute. It allegedly originated in Trastevere, the Roman haunt of these nocturnal ladies. And its name no doubt owes something to the fact that it is a piquant sauce, very quickly made.

NAPOLITANA
SERVES 4

1lb dried pasta
½ cup extra virgin olive oil
1 garlic clove, crushed
2lbs fresh ripe tomatoes,
 chopped or 2 - 14oz cans
 Italian plum tomatoes, chopped
1 tsp sugar
1 handful torn fresh basil
salt, black pepper

Cook pasta in a large pot of boiling, salted water until firm to the bite. While pasta is cooking, place oil, garlic, tomatoes, sugar, and basil in a skillet over medium high heat. Simmer rapidly until thickened, 10 minutes. Add salt and pepper to taste. Drain pasta. Add pasta to the hot sauce. Toss well to coat. Serve immediately.

WHICH PASTA?
Strands or tubes—spaghetti, penne, rigatoni.

THINK AHEAD
Make sauce up to 3 days in advance. Refrigerate.

ARRABBIATA
SERVES 4

½ cup extra virgin olive oil
1 medium onion, finely sliced
3 garlic cloves, sliced
1 tsp crushed red pepper flakes
2 - 14oz cans italian plum
 tomatoes, chopped
salt, black pepper
1lb dried pasta
2 tbsp torn fresh basil or flat-leaf
 parsley, optional

Heat oil in a skillet. Add onion, garlic, and red pepper flakes and cook, over medium high heat, stirring frequently, until soft and golden, 7 minutes. Add tomatoes and cook, stirring occasionally, until thickened, 15 minutes. Add salt and pepper to taste. Meanwhile, cook pasta in a large pot of boiling, salted water until firm to the bite. Drain. Add pasta with your choice of herb, if using, to the hot sauce. Toss to coat. Serve immediately.

WHICH PASTA?
Strands or tubes—spaghetti, penne, rigatoni.

THINK AHEAD
Make sauce up to 3 days in advance. Refrigerate.

COOKS' NOTE
The name of this sauce from Central Italy means "angry," because of the potency of its flavor.

QUICK COOK
FRESH TOMATO SAUCE

SERVES 4

1lb dried pasta
6 tbsp extra virgin olive oil
3 garlic cloves, crushed
1½ lbs ripe fresh
   tomatoes, peeled
   (optional) and cut into
   6 pieces

salt, black pepper
1 handful torn fresh basil
   leaves, optional
additional extra virgin
   olive oil to toss

Cook pasta in a large pot of boiling, salted water, until firm to the bite. While pasta is cooking, heat oil in a skillet. Add garlic and cook over medium heat until fragrant, 1 minute. Add tomatoes and cook, stirring frequently, until tomatoes are sizzling hot but still retaining their fresh flavor and bright color, about 5 minutes. Add salt and pepper to taste. Drain pasta. Add pasta, with the basil if using, to the hot sauce. Toss well to coat, adding 2 tbsp additional olive oil as needed. Serve immediately.

WHICH PASTA?
Strands or thin to medium ribbons—spaghetti, fettuccine, tagliatelle.

THINK AHEAD
All these variations are best made at least 8 hours in advance to allow the flavors to blend.

VARIATIONS
FRESH TOMATO SAUCE WITH PESTO
Omit basil. Add 3 tbsp simple basil pesto (see page 105) with the drained pasta to the hot sauce.

FRESH TOMATO WITH MOLTEN MOZZARELLA
Make sauce as directed. Turn down heat to low. Add 1 cup diced mozzarella to sauce and heat gently until it is just melting, about 1 minute. Omit the additional 2 tbsp olive oil. Finish as directed.

PIQUANT FRESH TOMATO
Add 8 sliced pitted black olives, such as kalamata or gaeta, 2 tsp capers, rinsed and drained, and ¼ tsp crushed red pepper flakes with the tomatoes to the skillet. Finish as directed.

FRESH TOMATO WITH RICOTTA
Make sauce as directed. Turn down heat to low. Add ½ cup ricotta to sauce and heat gently until warm through, 1 minute. Omit the additional 2 tbsp olive oil. Finish as directed.

SPICY FRESH TOMATO SAUCE
Add ¼ tsp crushed red pepper flakes with the garlic to the skillet. Finish as directed.

SLOW COOK
TOMATO AND MOZZARELLA AL FORNO

SERVES 4

2 tbsp extra virgin olive oil

2 cloves garlic, crushed

**2 - 14oz cans Italian plum tomatoes, chopped or
2lbs fresh tomatoes, seeded and chopped**

2 tsp fresh oregano or 1 tsp dried

salt, black pepper

1lb dried pasta

8oz mozzarella cheese, cut into 1-inch dice

**¾ cup freshly grated Parmesan, plus additional
to serve**

Preheat oven to 400°F

Heat oil in a skillet. Add garlic and cook over medium-high heat until fragrant, 1 minute. Add tomatoes and oregano and simmer rapidly, stirring occasionally, until thickened, 15 minutes. Add salt and pepper to taste. Remove and reserve 6 tbsp tomato sauce from the pan. Meanwhile, cook pasta in a large pot of boiling, salted water, until just firm to the bite. Drain, reserving ½ cup pasta water. Toss drained pasta with remaining sauce, adding reserved water as needed. Place half the pasta in an oiled 13 x 9 x 3-inch ovenproof dish. Cover with half the mozzarella and half the Parmesan. Top with remaining pasta. Cover with reserved tomato sauce and remaining mozzarella. Sprinkle with remaining Parmesan. Bake until golden and bubbling, 15 minutes.

WHICH PASTA?

Tubes or shapes—penne, rigatoni, fusilli.

THINK AHEAD

Assemble and leave to cool completely. Cover, unbaked, and refrigerate up to 8 hours in advance. Bake as directed. Alternatively, cover unbaked and freeze up to 3 weeks in advance. Defrost overnight in refrigerator. Cook in preheated 400°F oven for 30 minutes.

VARIATION

PAN-COOKED TOMATO AND MOZZARELLA

Make sauce as directed, but over low heat. Add mozzarella to the hot sauce and heat gently until just melting, 1 minute. Meanwhile, cook pasta in a large pot of boiling, salted water, until firm to the bite. Drain, reserving ½ cup pasta water. Add drained pasta with Parmesan to the hot sauce. Toss well to coat, adding reserved water as needed. Serve hot with extra Parmesan.

ROASTED TOMATO

SERVES 4

6 medium-sized fresh ripe tomatoes, halved
2 garlic cloves, crushed
¼ tsp crushed red pepper flakes
½ tsp dried oregano
salt, black pepper
3 tbsp extra virgin olive oil
2 tbsp balsamic vinegar
1lb dried pasta
2 tbsp freshly grated Parmesan, plus additional to serve
additional extra virgin olive oil

Preheat oven to 300°F. Place tomato halves cut side up in an oven tray. Sprinkle with garlic, red pepper flakes, oregano, salt, and pepper. Drizzle with oil and vinegar. Roast in oven until very soft and wilted, 1½ hours. Meanwhile, cook pasta in a large pot of boiling, salted water, until firm to the bite. Drain. Place drained pasta in a warm bowl and toss with Parmesan and 1–2 tbsp additional extra virgin olive oil. Place tomatoes on top. Serve immediately with additional Parmesan.

WHICH PASTA?
Strands or ribbons—spaghetti, linguine, fettuccine, tagliatelle, pappardelle.

THINK AHEAD
Roast tomatoes up to 1 day in advance. Cover and refrigerate. Reheat in preheated 400°F oven for 10 minutes.

VARIATIONS
ROASTED TOMATO WITH PESTO
Add 4 tbsp simple basil pesto (see page 105), in place of the Parmesan and oil, to the drained pasta.

ROASTED TOMATO WITH RICOTTA AND BASIL
Add a ½ cup ricotta and a handful of torn basil with the Parmesan to the drained pasta.

ROASTED TOMATO WITH CRISPY PANCETTA
Cook 4 unsmoked pancetta or bacon slices, turning frequently, in a skillet over medium-low heat until browned and crisp, 10 minutes. Drain on paper towels and cut into 1-inch wide strips. Add pancetta with the Parmesan to the drained pasta.

SLOW COOK
SIMMERED TOMATO

SERVES 4
¼ **cup extra virgin olive oil**
1 **medium onion, finely chopped**
1 **garlic clove, crushed**
2 - 14oz **cans plum tomatoes, chopped**
salt, black pepper
1lb **dried pasta**
freshly grated Parmesan to serve, optional

Place oil, onion, garlic, and tomatoes in a heavy-bottomed pot.
Bring to a fast simmer over medium heat. Turn heat to low and
simmer gently, stirring occasionally, until thick and deep red,
30–40 minutes. If the sauce becomes too dry and starts to stick,
add a few tablespoons of water. Add salt and pepper to taste.
Meanwhile, cook pasta in a large pot of boiling, salted water,
until firm to the bite. Drain. Add pasta to the hot sauce. Toss
well to coat. Serve immediately with Parmesan.

WHICH PASTA?
Strands and tubes—spaghettini, spaghetti, penne, rigatoni.

THINK AHEAD
Make sauce up to 3 days in advance. Cover and refrigerate. If making
variations with cream, add cream just before serving.

VARIATIONS
SIMMERED TOMATO WITH RED WINE AND ROSEMARY
Add ½ cup red wine and 2 tsp finely chopped fresh rosemary
with the onion, garlic, and tomatoes to the pot. Cook and serve
as directed.

SIMMERED TOMATO WITH AROMATICS
Add 1 finely chopped celery stalk and 1 finely chopped small
carrot with the onion, garlic, and tomatoes to the pan. Cook
and serve as directed.

SIMMERED TOMATO WITH CINNAMON AND BAY
Add ¼ tsp cinnamon and 1 dry or 2 fresh bay leaves with the
onion, garlic, and tomatoes to the pan. Cook and serve as
directed, removing the bay leaves before serving.

SIMMERED TOMATO WITH CREAM
Omit oil. Cook sauce as directed. Transfer to food processor;
pulse until smooth. Return to pan over medium heat. Stir in
½ cup heavy cream and cook until hot through, 1–2 minutes.
Serve as directed.

SIMMERED TOMATO WITH VODKA
Omit oil. Cook sauce as directed. Transfer to food processor;
pulse until smooth. Return to the pan over medium heat. Add
3 tbsp vodka and simmer rapidly to evaporate alcohol, 2 minutes.
Stir in ½ cup heavy cream and 2 tbsp butter and cook until
heated through, 1–2 minutes. Serve as directed.

PASTA WITH BUTTER AND CHEESE

CHEESE IN THE PASTA PANTRY

No pasta lover's pantry is complete without a wedge of Parmesan in the refrigerator. Always buy Parmesan in a piece, never pre-grated. It's best to buy a wedge that weighs no more than 8–10oz, since a larger piece will probably dry out before you use it up. Store wrapped in foil in the warmest part of the refrigerator. If it does dry out, try wrapping it in a piece of damp cheesecloth to remoisten. Parmesan can be frozen and it will retain its flavor well, but it will become too crumbly to grate when defrosted.

We always buy Italian Parmesan and, whenever possible, *Parmigiano-Reggiano*. Although more expensive, it is unquestionably superior in flavor and texture. We like to present Parmesan at the table in a manageable piece with a small hand grater and allow everyone to enjoy freshly grating their own additional cheese. Otherwise, grate it first in the kitchen and serve it in a bowl. *Pecorino Romano* is a tangy, salty sheep's milk cheese which is also suitable for grating. It is traditionally served with pasta dishes originating from Southern Italy, where pungent flavors dominate. When called

for in a recipe, it is because the distinctively sharp taste of Pecorino is the best complement to the sauce. And, although we do list grated Parmesan as an alternative, we urge you to seek out Pecorino cheese from Italian specialty and gourmet stores to serve when it is the most appropriate choice for the recipe.

Gorgonzola is a creamy colored, blue-veined cheese with a flavor that varies from mildly tangy to piquant. When buying Gorgonzola for pasta, remember that the creamier the consistency, the mellower the flavor.

When buying mozzarella at the supermarket, always choose whole milk "fresh" mozzarella that comes in a squashed, ball shape and is sold surrounded by water in plastic bags. Never buy the rubbery blocks of mozzarella. Real mozzarella is made from the milk of the Italian water buffalo and has a fresher flavor than mozzarella made from cow's milk. But for cooking, the superior buffalo mozzarella is not essential.

NO COOK
BUTTER AND PARMESAN

SERVES 4

1lb dried pasta
9 tbsp butter, cut into cubes
1¼ cups freshly grated Parmesan
salt, black pepper
additional freshly grated Parmesan, to serve

Cook pasta in a large pot of boiling, salted water, until firm
to the bite. Drain. Return pasta to the warm pasta pot.
Add butter to the pasta. Toss well to coat. Add Parmesan
and salt and pepper to taste. Serve immediately with
additional Parmesan.

WHICH PASTA?
Strands or ribbons—spaghetti, tagliolini, fettuccine, tagliatelle, pappardelle.

COOKS' NOTE
Don't hold back on the black pepper—this dish is best with generous amounts.

VARIATIONS
BUTTER, PARMESAN, AND HAM
Add 4 slices ham, cut into short, fine strips, 1 inch long and
¼ inch wide, to pasta with butter. Finish as directed.

BUTTER, PARMESAN, AND PARSLEY
Add 2 tbsp finely chopped fresh flat-leaf parsley to pasta with
the butter. Finish as directed.

BUTTER, PARMESAN, AND ASPARAGUS
Cook 3 cups small asparagus tips in boiling, salted water until
just tender, 2–3 minutes. Drain and add immediately to hot pasta
with the butter. Toss gently to avoid crushing. Finish as directed.

BUTTER, PARMESAN, AND PEAS
Cook 1 cup tiny frozen peas in boiling, salted water until just
tender, 2 minutes. Drain and add immediately to hot pasta
with the butter. Finish as directed.

NO COOK
CREAM AND PARMESAN

SERVES 4

1 cup heavy cream
2 egg yolks, beaten
¾ cup freshly grated Parmesan
1lb dried pasta
salt, black pepper
additional freshly grated Parmesan
to serve

Mix cream, egg yolks, and Parmesan in a bowl until combined. Meanwhile, cook pasta in a large pot of boiling, salted water, until firm to the bite. Drain pasta, reserving ½ cup pasta water. Return pasta to the warm pasta pot. Add cream mixture and toss well to coat, adding reserved water as needed. Add salt and pepper to taste. Serve immediately with additional Parmesan.

WHICH PASTA?
Ribbons—fettuccine, tagliatelle, pappardelle.

NO COOK
THREE CHEESE

SERVES 4

1lb dried pasta
1⅛ cups freshly grated Parmesan
1 cup grated emmental, Gruyère, or Edam
1 cup grated mozzarella, Fontina, or provolone
8 tbsp (1 stick) butter, cut into cubes
black pepper

Cook pasta in a large pot of boiling, salted water, until firm to the bite. Drain, reserving ½ cup pasta water. Add butter to the warm pasta pot and stir until melted. Return drained pasta with Parmesan and your choice of cheeses. Toss well to coat, adding reserved water as needed. Add pepper to taste. Serve immediately.

WHICH PASTA?
Medium tubes or shapes—penne, macaroni, fusilli, conchiglie.

NO COOK
GORGONZOLA AND RICOTTA

SERVES 4

1lb dried pasta
4 tbsp crumbled Gorgonzola
½ cup ricotta
4 tbsp (½ stick) butter
salt, black pepper
additional crumbled Gorgonzola to serve

Cook pasta in a large pot of boiling, salted water, until firm to the bite. Drain, reserving ½ cup pasta water. Return pasta with Gorgonzola, ricotta, and butter to the warm pasta pot. Toss well to coat, adding reserved water as needed. Add salt and pepper to taste. Serve immediately, sprinkled with an additional 2 tbsp Gorgonzola.

WHICH PASTA?
Medium tubes or shapes—cavatelli, penne, macaroni, fusilli, conchiglie.

VARIATIONS

GORGONZOLA, RICOTTA, AND BABY SPINACH
Add 2 handfuls baby spinach leaves to the drained pasta with the Gorgonzola and ricotta. Finish as directed.

GORGONZOLA, RICOTTA, AND BASIL
Add 1 handful fresh basil leaves to the drained pasta with the Gorgonzola and ricotta. Finish as directed.

GORGONZOLA, RICOTTA, AND ARUGULA
Add 2 handfuls arugula leaves to the drained pasta with the Gorgonzola and ricotta. Finish as directed.

QUICK COOK
GORGONZOLA CREAM

SERVES 4

1lb dried pasta
2 tbsp butter
1 cup crumbled Gorgonzola
3 tbsp milk
¾ cup heavy cream
salt, black pepper

Cook pasta in a large pot of boiling, salted water, until firm to the bite. While pasta is cooking, melt butter in a skillet over low heat. Add Gorgonzola and milk and warm gently, stirring constantly, until melted, 2 minutes. Stir in cream and warm gently until hot through, 1 minute. Add salt and pepper to taste. Drain pasta. Add pasta to the hot sauce. Toss well to coat. Serve immediately.

WHICH PASTA?
Ribbons—tagliolini, fettuccine, tagliatelle, pappardelle.

QUICK COOK
LEMON, BASIL, AND MASCARPONE

SERVES 4

1lb dried pasta
5 tbsp fresh lemon juice
1 tsp grated lemon zest
1 cup mascarpone
salt, black pepper
1 handful torn fresh basil

Cook pasta in a large pot of boiling, salted water, until firm to the bite. While pasta is cooking, place mascarpone, with 2–3 tablespoons of pasta water, in a skillet over medium low heat. When melted and smooth, gradually add lemon juice and zest. Warm gently, stirring constantly, until heated through, 3–4 minutes. Salt and pepper to taste. Drain pasta, reserving ½ cup pasta water. Add pasta with basil to sauce. Toss well to coat, adding reserved water as needed. Serve immediately.

WHICH PASTA?
Ribbons or strands—linguine, fettuccine, tagliatelle.

COOKS' NOTE
Mascarpone is an Italian cream cheese; here its richness is lightened by the lemon and the basil.

QUICK COOK
FOUR CHEESES AL FORNO

SERVES 4

1lb dried pasta
5 tbsp butter
½ cup Gruyère, cut into
 ½-inch cubes
½ cup Fontina, cut into
 ½-inch cubes

¾ cup mozzarella, cut into
 ½-inch cubes
6 tbsp freshly grated Parmesan
pinch cayenne pepper
additional freshly grated
 Parmesan to top
1 tbsp dried breadcrumbs

Preheat oven to 400°F.
Cook pasta in a large pot of boiling, salted water, until just firm to the bite.
Drain, reserving ½ cup pasta water. Return pasta with butter to warm pasta pot
and stir to coat. Add Gruyère, Fontina, mozzarella, Parmesan, and cayenne. Mix
thoroughly until the cheese is melting but not completely melted. Place in a buttered
13 x 9-inch ovenproof baking dish. Sprinkle with 1 tbsp additional Parmesan and
breadcrumbs. Bake until just golden and crusty, 10–15 minutes. Let stand for
5 minutes before serving.

WHICH PASTA?
Medium tubes or shapes—penne, macaroni, fusilli, conchiglie.

THINK AHEAD
Assemble up to 1 day in advance. Cover, unbaked, and refrigerate. Allow an extra 5 minutes in the oven when
cooking from cold.

QUICK COOK
GOLDEN SAFFRON

SERVES 4

4 tbsp (½ stick) butter
1 shallot, finely chopped
pinch saffron threads, soaked in
 ¼ cup boiling water
½ cup dry white wine
½ cup heavy cream
salt, black pepper
1lb dried pasta

Melt butter in a skillet over medium
heat. Add shallot and cook, stirring
frequently, until soft, 5 minutes. Add
saffron, saffron water, and wine and
simmer rapidly until reduced by half,
5 minutes. Add cream and cook until
thickened, 1 minute. Add salt and pepper
to taste. Meanwhile, cook pasta in a
large pot of boiling, salted water, until
firm to the bite. Drain, reserving ½ cup
pasta water. Add pasta to the hot sauce.
Toss well to coat, adding reserved water
as needed. Serve immediately.

WHICH PASTA?
Medium to wide ribbons—fettuccine, tagliatelle,
pappardelle.

QUICK COOK
ALL'ALFREDO

SERVES 4

1lb dried pasta
2 tbsp butter
1 cup heavy cream
¾ cup freshly grated Parmesan
salt, black pepper
additional freshly grated Parmesan
** to serve**

Cook pasta in a large pot of boiling, salted water, until firm to the bite. While pasta is cooking, place butter and cream in a skillet over medium low heat. Heat through, then simmer gently until the mixture is just thickened, 1–2 minutes. Add salt and pepper to taste. Drain pasta. Add pasta with Parmesan to the hot sauce. Toss well to coat. Serve immediately with additional Parmesan.

WHICH PASTA?
Medium to wide ribbons—fettuccine, tagliatelle, pappardelle.

COOKS' NOTE
Fettuccine is the traditional pasta to serve with this famous sauce. Alfredo was the owner of a restaurant in Rome where the great and the good flocked in the 1950s and 60s. He used to give a final toss to the tagliatelle with a large gold fork and spoon before setting the dish on the tables.

Pasta with Mushrooms

MUSHROOMS IN THE PASTA PANTRY

The very best and most authentic mushrooms for pasta are the meaty-textured, earthy-flavored porcini and boletus varieties, but cultivated cremini and portobello mushrooms, especially in combination with dried porcini, are an acceptable and economical substitutes. White button mushrooms are not. To boost and enhance the flavor of cultivated mushrooms, mix ¾ cup of dried porcini with 8oz fresh mushrooms. Never wash fresh mushrooms under running water. To clean, use a damp cloth or piece of paper towel and wipe away any dirt. When buying dried porcini, choose the packages with the largest mushroom pieces, since they come from the caps.

The smaller, crumbly bits are the stalks and have less flavor. Porcini should be reconstituted in hot water for a minimum of 30 minutes. Try the following alternative method when making creamy mushroom sauces: place the porcini in a small pan with equal amounts of water and milk to cover. Bring to a boil and boil for 1 minute. When using either method, do not stir, so the sediment can settle. Remove from heat and let soak for 20 minutes. Use the soaked mushrooms and milky soaking liquid in the sauce. Be careful, when pouring sauce, to leave sediment behind. Dried porcini will keep in a cool, dark place for up to 1 year.

QUICK COOK
WILD MUSHROOM PERSILLADE

SERVES 4

2 tbsp extra virgin olive oil
2 garlic cloves, finely chopped
2 shallots, finely chopped
1lb wild mushrooms, sliced
salt, black pepper
1lb dried pasta
¼ cup freshly grated Parmesan
3 tbsp finely chopped fresh flat-leaf
parsley
additional freshly grated Parmesan

Heat oil in a skillet. Add garlic and shallots and cook over medium-high heat until fragrant, 1 minute. Add mushrooms and cook, stirring frequently, until tender and colored, 10 minutes. Add salt and pepper to taste. Meanwhile, cook pasta in a large pot of boiling, salted water, until firm to the bite. Drain, reserving ½ cup pasta water. Add pasta with Parmesan and parsley to the hot mushrooms. Toss well to coat, adding reserved water as needed. Serve immediately with additional Parmesan.

WHICH PASTA?
Strands or thin to medium ribbons - spaghetti, fettuccine, tagliatelle.

COOKS' NOTE
There are many varieties of wild mushrooms. You can use a single variety or a mixture for this recipe. Our preferred choice would be fresh porcini or chanterelles, but portobello mushrooms and cremini mushrooms have a good rich flavor, are easy to find, and inexpensive.

QUICK COOK
MUSHROOM, WHITE WINE, AND CREAM

SERVES 4

1lb dried pasta
2 tbsp butter
1 tbsp extra virgin olive oil
1 garlic clove, finely chopped
8oz cremini or wild mushrooms
  (see page 56), finely sliced
¼ cup white wine
½ cup heavy cream
salt, black pepper
freshly grated Parmesan to serve

Cook pasta in a large pot of boiling, salted water, until firm to the bite. While pasta is cooking, melt butter with oil in a skillet over medium high heat. Add garlic and mushrooms and cook, stirring frequently, until just colored, 5 minutes. Add wine and simmer until just evaporated. Stir in cream and simmer gently until just thickened, 1–2 minutes. Drain pasta, reserving about ½ cup pasta water. Add pasta to the hot sauce. Toss well to coat, adding reserved water as needed. Serve immediately with Parmesan.

WHICH PASTA?
Medium to wide ribbons—fettuccine, tagliatelle, pappardelle.

COOKS' NOTE
Use portobello or cremini mushrooms for this dish if wild mushrooms are beyond your budget or not available. For a superlative dish with an even deeper mushroom flavor, we strongly recommend adding dried porcini mushrooms (see variation below).

VARIATION
PORCINI, WHITE WINE, AND CREAM SAUCE
Soak 1 cup of dried porcini in ½ cup hot water (see page 156). Finely chop and add to the hot pan with the garlic and fresh mushrooms. Cook as directed. Carefully add the reserved mushroom soaking liquid, leaving any sediment in the bowl. Add the wine. Finish as directed.

QUICK COOK
TOMATOES WITH PORCINI

SERVES 4

1cup dried porcini mushrooms
2 tbsp butter
3 tbsp extra virgin olive oil
1 small onion, finely chopped
1 garlic clove, finely chopped
1 - 14oz can Italian plum tomatoes, chopped
1lb dried pasta
freshly grated Parmesan to serve

Soak, but do not stir, the dried porcini (see page 156). Drain mushroom pieces, reserving the soaking liquid, and finely chop. Set aside. Melt butter with olive oil in a skillet over medium heat. Add onion and garlic and cook until softened, 5 minutes. Add tomatoes and cook, stirring occasionally, until thickened, 10 minutes. Adjust heat to low. Add mushrooms and reserved soaking liquid, leaving any sediment in the bowl, and simmer gently for 5 minutes. Meanwhile, cook pasta in a large pot of boiling, salted water, until firm to the bite. Drain. Add pasta to the hot sauce. Toss well to coat. Serve immediately with Parmesan.

WHICH PASTA?
Strands, tubes or shapes—spaghetti, penne, fusilli.

THINK AHEAD
Make sauce up to 3 days in advance. Cover and refrigerate.

SLOW COOK
MUSHROOM AL FORNO

SERVES 4–6

1 cup dried porcini mushrooms
FOR BECHAMEL
5 tbsp butter
4½ tbsp all-purpose flour
3⅛ cups milk
salt, black pepper, nutmeg
FOR SAUCE
1 tbsp extra virgin olive oil
2 tbsp butter
8oz cremini or wild mushrooms, finely sliced
1 tsp fresh thyme or ½ tsp dried
2 garlic cloves, crushed
1lb dried pasta
6 tbsp freshly grated Parmesan

Soak, but do not stir, the porcini (see page 156). Drain, reserving the soaking liquid, and finely chop. Set aside. Preheat oven to 400°F.
For bechamel, melt butter over medium heat in a heavy saucepan. Whisk in flour and cook until foaming, about 1 minute. Remove from heat and gradually pour in milk, whisking constantly. Return to heat and cook, whisking constantly, until sauce thickens, about 2 minutes. Bring to a boil and remove from heat. Add salt, pepper, and nutmeg to taste. Carefully stir in mushrooms and reserved soaking liquid, leaving any sediment in the bowl.
In a small pan, melt butter with oil and add fresh mushrooms, thyme, and garlic. Cook over medium high heat, stirring frequently, until mushrooms are just colored, 5 minutes. Remove from heat. Stir into bechamel.
Meanwhile, cook pasta in a large pot of boiling, salted water, until just firm to the bite. Drain. Combine drained pasta and mushroom bechamel. Add 2 tbsp of the Parmesan. Toss. Place in a buttered 13 x 9-inch ovenproof dish. Sprinkle the remaining Parmesan over top. Bake until golden and bubbling, 10 minutes. Let stand for 5 minutes before serving.

WHICH PASTA?
Tubes or shells—penne, macaroni, rigatoni, conchiglie.

THINK AHEAD
Assemble and let cool completely unbaked. Cover, unbaked, and refrigerate up to 1 day in advance. Alternatively, freeze up to 3 weeks in advance. Defrost overnight in refrigerator. Cook in preheated 400°F oven for 30 minutes.

PASTA WITH SEAFOOD

NO COOK
SMOKED SALMON, VODKA, AND DILL

SERVES 4

1lb dried pasta
4 tbsp (½ stick) butter
1 tsp vodka
½ cup sour cream
salt, black pepper
7oz smoked salmon, cut
  into strips
1 tbsp dill sprigs

Cook pasta in a large pot of boiling, salted water, until firm to the bite. Drain, reserving ½ cup pasta water. Return drained pasta to the warm pasta pot. Add butter, vodka, and half the sour cream. Toss well to coat, adding reserved water as needed. Add salt and pepper to taste. Top with salmon, remaining sour cream, and dill. Serve immediately.

WHICH PASTA?
Thin to medium ribbons—linguine, fettuccine, tagliatelle.

NO COOK
TUNA WITH LEMON AND CAPERS

SERVES 4

1lb dried pasta
2 - 6oz cans tuna in oil,
  drained and flaked
8oz (about 1¾ cups) cherry tomatoes
1 tbsp drained capers
handful fresh basil, torn
½ tsp lemon zest
2 tbsp fresh lemon juice
6 tbsp extra virgin olive oil
salt, black pepper

Cook pasta in a large pot of boiling, salted water, until firm to the bite if serving hot. If serving this dish as a salad, slightly undercook the pasta. Drain. Return drained pasta to the warm pasta pot. Add tuna, tomatoes, capers, basil, lemon, and oil. Toss well to coat. Add pepper to taste. Serve immediately or at room temperature.

WHICH PASTA
Tubes or shells—conchiglie, gnocchi, rigatoni.

THINK AHEAD
Make up to 1 day in advance if serving as a pasta salad. Cover and refrigerate. Bring to room temperature before serving.

NO COOK
SALMON CAVIAR WITH BUTTER AND CHIVES

SERVES 4

1lb dried pasta
6 tbsp butter
2 tbsp finely chopped chives
3½oz salmon roe
salt, black pepper

Cook pasta in a large pot of boiling, salted water, until firm to the bite. Drain, reserving about ½ cup pasta water. Return pasta with butter and chives to the warm pasta pot. Toss well to coat, adding reserved water as needed. Add salmon roe and toss carefully to avoid crushing roe. Add salt and pepper to taste. Serve immediately.

WHICH PASTA?
Thin strands—capellini, spaghettini, paglia e fieno.

COOKS' NOTE
If using capellini or *paglia e fieno*—also called "straw and hay"—be sure to cook in plenty of boiling water. Stir with a long wooden fork as soon as the pasta slides into the water, and drain when pasta is still slightly undercooked.

NO COOK
SHRIMP WITH LEMON AND BASIL

SERVES 4

1lb dried pasta
¾lb cooked, peeled medium shrimp
2 garlic cloves, finely chopped
½ red onion, finely chopped
2 tbsp fresh lemon juice
½ tsp crushed red pepper flakes
5 tbsp extra virgin olive oil
12 cherry tomatoes, halved
2 tbsp chopped fresh basil
salt, black pepper

Cook pasta in a large pot of boiling, salted water, until firm to the bite if serving hot If serving this dish as a salad, slightly undercook the pasta. While pasta is cooking, combine shrimp, garlic, onion, red pepper flakes, lemon juice, oil, tomatoes, and basil in a bowl. Drain pasta. Return pasta, shrimp, and tomato mixture to the warm pasta pot. Toss well to coat. Add salt and pepper to taste. Serve immediately or at room temperature.

WHICH PASTA?
Thin strands or medium shells—spaghetti, gnocchi, conchiglie.

THINK AHEAD
Make up to 8 hours in advance if serving as a salad. Cover and refrigerate. Return to room temperature before serving.

COOKS' NOTE
For an authentic Italian flavor, use a peppery olive oil from Tuscany or Umbria.

QUICK COOK
SCALLOPS WITH GARLIC AND CRISP CRUMBS

SERVES 4

1lb dried pasta
½ cup extra virgin olive oil
2 garlic cloves, finely chopped
2 tbsp chopped fresh flat-leaf parsley
½ cup dried breadcrumbs (see page 160)
½ tsp crushed red pepper flakes
12 sea scallops, cut into quarters, or 24 bay scallops
salt, black pepper

Cook pasta in a large pot of boiling, salted water, until firm to the bite. While pasta is cooking, heat oil in a skillet. Add garlic, parsley, crumbs, and red pepper flakes and cook over a high heat, 1 minute. Add scallops and cook, stirring constantly, until just turning opaque, 1–2 minutes. Add salt and pepper to taste. Drain pasta and add to hot pan. Toss well to coat. Serve immediately.

WHICH PASTA?
Thin to medium ribbons—linguine, fettuccine.

COOKS' NOTE
The difficulty of this sauce lies in the timing. The pasta must be ready when the scallops are ready. Scallops become tough if overcooked. A sweet olive oil, preferably Ligurian, will best complement the scallops' natural sweetness.

QUICK COOK
WHITE CLAM SAUCE

SERVES 4

2lbs littleneck clams, in shells
½ cup dry white wine
1lb dried pasta
4 tbsp extra virgin olive oil
2 garlic cloves, finely chopped
¼ tsp crushed red pepper flakes
2 tbsp finely chopped fresh flat-leaf parsley
additional extra virgin olive oil
salt, black pepper

Scrub clams under running water. Discard any that are broken or not tightly closed. Place clams with wine in a large pot with a lid on. Steam over medium heat until shells are open, shaking pot occasionally to ensure even cooking, about 5–6 minutes. Use a slotted spoon to lift out clams, and set aside. Discard any that do not open. Tip the pot and slowly pour out the clear clam and wine juices to reserve, being careful to leave the sandy residue in the pot. Discard residue. Remove clams from shells and reserve, discarding shells.

Cook pasta in large pot of boiling, salted water, until firm to the bite. While pasta is cooking, heat oil in a skillet. Add garlic, red pepper flakes, and parsley. Cook over medium heat until fragrant, 1 minute. Add reserved clam juices and boil vigorously for 1 minute. Remove from heat.

Drain pasta. Add pasta to hot clam juices. Return to heat and cook, tossing constantly for 1 minute. Add clams and 2 tbsp additional olive oil and toss well. Add salt and pepper to taste. Serve immediately.

WHICH PASTA?
Strands or thin ribbons—spaghettini, spaghetti, linguine.

COOKS' NOTE
A simple variation for this recipe is to replace clams with mussels. Cook as directed above. You could leave a handful of mussels in their bottom shells as a garnish.

QUICK COOK
TUNA AND TOMATO

SERVES 4

6 tbsp extra virgin olive oil
1 small onion, finely chopped
2 garlic cloves, crushed
1 - 14oz can Italian plum tomatoes, chopped
1 - 6oz can tuna in oil, drained and flaked
salt, black pepper
1lb dried pasta

Heat oil in a skillet. Add onion and garlic and cook, stirring constantly over medium high heat, until softened, 5 minutes. Add tomatoes. Simmer rapidly until just thickened, 10 minutes. Add tuna and cook until hot through, 3 minutes. Add salt and pepper to taste. Meanwhile, cook pasta in a large pot of boiling, salted water, until firm to the bite. Drain. Add pasta to the hot sauce. Toss well to coat. Serve immediately.

WHICH PASTA?
Strands, thin ribbons or tubes—spaghetti, linguine, or penne.

THINK AHEAD
Make sauce up to 2 days in advance. Cover and refrigerate.

VARIATION
PIQUANT TUNA WITH TOMATOES
Add 1 tbsp rinsed capers and 12 sliced pitted black olives, such as kalamata or gaeta, to the pan with the tuna. Finish as directed.

CHILI SQUID

SERVES 4

1lb dried pasta
5 tbsp extra virgin olive oil
4 garlic cloves, finely sliced
½ tsp crushed red pepper flakes
**12oz squid, cleaned and cut
  into ½-inch rings**
2 tbsp fresh lemon juice
**2 tbsp finely chopped fresh
  flat-leaf parsley**
salt, black pepper

Cook pasta in a large pot of boiling, salted water, until firm to the bite. hile pasta is cooking, heat oil in a skillet. Add garlic and red pepper flakes and cook over high heat until just golden, 1–2 minutes. Add squid and cook, stirring constantly, until opaque, 2–3 minutes. Add lemon juice, parsley, and salt and pepper to taste. Drain pasta. Add pasta to the hot squid. Toss well to coat. Serve immediately.

WHICH PASTA?
Strands or thin ribbons—spaghetti, linguine.

COOKS' NOTE
Squid needs to be cooked either quickly over high heat or slowly over low heat to avoid a tough, rubbery texture. In this recipe, be sure to combine with the pasta as soon as the squid is cooked.

VARIATION
CHILI SHRIMP
Replace squid with 12oz raw peeled medium shrimp. Cook as directed until shrimp are pink and firm, 3–4 minutes. Finish as directed.

SMOKED SALMON WITH WHITE WINE, CREAM, AND CHIVES

SERVES 4

4 tbsp (½ stick) butter
2 shallots, finely chopped
1 cup white wine
¾ cup heavy cream
grated zest of ½ lemon
2 tbsp fresh lemon juice

2 tbsp chopped fresh chives
**7oz smoked salmon slices, cut
  into strips**
salt, black pepper
1lb dried pasta
4 tsp salmon roe, optional

Melt butter in a skillet over medium-low heat. Add shallots and cook, stirring occasionally, until soft, 5 minutes. Add wine and simmer until reduced by half, 3 minutes. Add cream, lemon zest, juice, chives, and salmon. Warm over medium-low heat, without boiling, until hot through, 1 minute. Add salt and pepper to taste. Meanwhile, cook pasta in a large pot of boiling, salted water, until firm to the bite. Drain, reserving ½ cup pasta water. Add pasta to the hot sauce. Toss well to coat, adding reserved water as needed. Top with salmon roe, if using. Serve immediately.

WHICH PASTA?
Thin to medium ribbons—tagliolini, fettuccine, tagliatelle.

QUICK COOK
SCALLOPS WITH CREME FRAICHE AND DILL

SERVES 4

1lb dried pasta
4 tbsp (½ stick) butter
4 scallions, finely sliced
8 sea scallops, cut into quarters
3 tbsp sour cream, crème fraîche, or plain yogurt
2 tbsp chopped fresh dill
salt, black pepper

Cook pasta in a large pot of boiling, salted water, until firm to the bite. While pasta is cooking, melt butter in a skillet over medium heat. Add scallions and cook, stirring frequently, until soft, 3 minutes. Add scallops and cook, stirring constantly, until just turning opaque, 1-2 minutes. Add sour cream, crème fraîche, or plain yogurt, and dill. Continue cooking until heated through, 1 minute. Drain pasta, reserving ½ cup pasta water. Add pasta to hot sauce. Toss well to coat, adding reserved water as needed. Add salt and pepper to taste. Serve immediately.

WHICH PASTA?
Thin to medium ribbons—linguine, tagliolini, fettuccine, tagliatelle.

QUICK COOK

SPICY GARLIC SHRIMP WITH CHERRY TOMATOES

SERVES 4

1lb dried pasta
5 tbsp extra virgin olive oil
½ tsp crushed red pepper flakes
4 garlic cloves, finely chopped
1lb raw medium shrimp, shelled
8oz cherry tomatoes, halved
2 tbsp chopped fresh flat-leaf parsley
salt, black pepper

Cook pasta in a large pot of boiling, salted water, until just firm to the bite. Heat oil in a skillet. Add red pepper flakes and garlic and cook over high heat until pale gold, 1 minute. Add shrimp and cook, stirring constantly, until just turning pink, 1 minute. Add tomatoes and cook, stirring constantly, until tomatoes are hot and wilted and shrimp are firm, 2–3 minutes. Add salt and pepper to taste. Drain pasta. Add pasta with parsley to hot sauce. Toss well to coat. Serve immediately.

WHICH PASTA?
Strands and thin ribbons—spaghettini, spaghetti, linguine.

VARIATION

SPICY GARLIC SCALLOPS

Replace shrimp with 12oz sea scallops, halved. Cook as directed until just opaque, 2–3 minutes. Finish as directed.

SLOW COOK
RED MUSSEL SAUCE

SERVES 4

FOR TOMATO SAUCE
¼ cup extra virgin olive oil
2 garlic cloves, finely chopped
¼ tsp crushed red pepper flakes
1 - 14oz can Italian plum tomatoes, chopped, or
  1lb fresh ripe tomatoes, peeled and chopped
salt, black pepper

2lbs mussels
5 tbsp white wine
1lb dried pasta
2 tbsp fresh flat-leaf parsley, chopped

Heat oil in a skillet. Add garlic and red pepper flakes and cook over medium-high heat until just golden, 6 minutes. Add tomatoes. Simmer rapidly, stirring occasionally, until thick, 15 minutes. Add salt and pepper to taste.
Meanwhile, scrub mussels under running water. Discard any that are broken or not tightly closed. Place mussels and wine in a large pot with a lid on. Steam over medium heat, shaking occasionally, until shells are open, 5–6 minutes. Remove mussels with a slotted spoon and set aside. Discard any that do not open. Tip the pot and slowly pour out the clear mussel and wine juices to reserve, being careful to leave the sandy residue in the pot. Discard residue.
Meanwhile, cook pasta in a large pot of boiling, salted water, until firm to the bite. Drain pasta and add with mussels, mussel juices, and parsley to the hot sauce. Toss gently.
Serve immediately.

WHICH PASTA?
Strands or thin ribbons—spaghettini, spaghetti, linguine.

THINK AHEAD
Make tomato sauce up to 3 days in advance. Cover and refrigerate. Reheat before combining with mussels and pasta as directed.

COOKS' NOTE
For a more elegant presentation, remove and discard the empty half of the mussel shells.

VARIATION
RED CLAM SAUCE
Replace mussels with 2lbs littleneck clams in shells. Cook as directed.

SLOW COOK
SEAFOOD EXTRAVAGANZA

SERVES 4–6

1lb mussels or littleneck clams in shells
½ cup white wine
5 tbsp extra virgin olive oil
4 garlic cloves, crushed
8 raw medium shrimp with shells
4 medium squid, cleaned and cut
  into ½-inch rings
4 cooked crayfish
4 medium tomatoes, peeled, seeded,
  and diced
1 fresh red chile, such as serrano, finely sliced or
  ½–1 tsp red chile flakes
salt, black pepper
1lb dried pasta
1 handful whole fresh basil leaves
additional extra virgin olive oil for drizzling

Scrub mussels or clams under running water. Discard any that are broken or not tightly closed. Place wine and mussels or clams in a large, heavy-bottomed pot with a lid over medium high heat. Cook, shaking pan frequently, until shells open, 5 minutes. Remove mussels or clams with a slotted spoon and reserve. Discard any that do not open. Tip pot and slowly pour out clear seafood juices to reserve, being careful to leave sandy residue in the pot. Discard residue. Rinse and dry pot.
Heat oil in the pot over high heat. Add garlic and shrimp and cook, stirring constantly, until the shrimp are just turning pink, 2 minutes. Add the squid, crayfish, tomatoes, and chile. Cook, stirring constantly, until the squid is just opaque, 3–4 minutes. Add reserved seafood juices and heat through, 30 seconds. Add salt and pepper to taste. Remove from heat.
Meanwhile, cook pasta in a large pot of boiling, salted water, until firm to the bite. Drain. Add pasta with basil to the hot sauce. Toss gently to coat. Drizzle over about 1–2 tbsp additional olive oil. Serve immediately.

WHICH PASTA?
Thin strands or ribbons—spaghettini, spaghetti, or linguine.

COOKS' NOTE
For cooking you can use any good extra virgin oil, but for the final drizzle we suggest a peppery extra virgin oil from Puglia or from Tuscany.

PASTA WITH MEAT

MEAT IN THE PASTA PANTRY

Pancetta is an Italian bacon, but it has a distinctly different flavor from regular bacon because it is cured differently. For pasta, buy flat pancetta in a slab, not the rolled version. Unsmoked bacon can be used as a substitute, but for authentic Italian flavor we urge you to seek out pancetta from Italian specialty or gourmet stores. Buy several pieces about 2oz each cut into ¼–½-inch slices. Wrap separately and store in the freezer for up to 3 months. This way you will always have the real thing on hand when it is called for.

Prosciutto is a specially cured Italian ham that comes from the hind thigh of the pig and is air-cured for over a year. This long process of air-curing gives it a distinctively sweet flavor and delicate rosy color. Buy prosciutto sliced to order and avoid the packages of presliced meat wherever possible. Store it well wrapped in the refrigerator for no more than 3 days.

There is an old adage from Parma that says: *Grasso e magro non del tutto, ecco il pregio del prosciutto*. This means that prosciutto must have the right balance of fat and meat. When buying, look for prosciutto with a generous proportion of fat, since this contributes as much to the flavor as the meat part.

The best sausage to use for making pasta sauces is Luganega, a sweet medium-ground sausage. If you cannot find it, use a sweet Italian sausage with a very high percentage of pork meat.

QUICK COOK
PROSCIUTTO
AND CREAM

SERVES 4

1lb dried pasta
4 tbsp (½ stick) butter
7oz prosciutto slices, cut
  into strips ½-inch wide
½ small onion, finely chopped
¼ cup white wine
½ cup heavy cream
salt, black pepper
¼ cup freshly grated Parmesan, plus
  additional to serve

Cook pasta in a large pot of boiling,
salted water, until firm to the bite.
While pasta is cooking, melt butter in
a skillet over medium-low heat. Add
prosciutto strips and onion and cook,
stirring frequently, until onion is soft,
4–5 minutes. Add wine and raise heat
to medium high. Simmer until just
evaporated. Add cream and cook until
just thickened, 1 minute. Remove from
heat. Add salt and pepper to taste. Drain
pasta, reserving ½ cup pasta water. Add
pasta with Parmesan to the hot sauce.
Toss well to coat, adding reserved water
as needed. Serve immediately with
additional Parmesan.

WHICH PASTA?
Medium ribbons—fettuccine, tagliatelle.

QUICK COOK
PIZZAIOLA

SERVES 4

2 tbsp extra virgin olive oil
1¾lbs rump steak, cut into strips 2 inches long
  and ½inch wide
1 - 14oz can chopped italian plum tomatoes
2 garlic cloves, crushed
2 tsp fresh oregano or 1 tsp dried
2 tbsp capers, drained and rinsed
¼ cup pitted, sliced black olives, such as kalamata or gaeta
1lb dried pasta
1 tbsp finely chopped fresh flat-leaf parsley

Heat oil in a skillet. Add steak and cook over high heat until browned all over, 3 minutes. Remove from skillet with slotted spoon, cover to keep warm, and reserve. Reduce heat to medium high. Add tomatoes, garlic, oregano, capers, and olives. Simmer rapidly, stirring occasionally, until thickened, 10 minutes. Remove pan from heat. Return steak to the skillet to keep warm. Meanwhile, cook pasta in a large pot of boiling, salted water. Drain. Add pasta with parsley to the hot sauce. Toss well to coat. Serve immediately.

WHICH PASTA?
Strands—spaghetti, spaghettini.

COOKS' NOTE
This sauce is so called because it contains oregano which, with tomato, is one of the traditional ingredients for pizza.

QUICK COOK
CRISPY PANCETTA AND SCALLIONS

SERVES 4

8 pancetta or bacon slices, smoked or unsmoked
2 tbsp butter
2 tbsp extra virgin olive oil
4 scallions, sliced
1lb dried pasta
¼ cup freshly grated Parmesan
salt, black pepper
additional freshly grated Parmesan to serve

Cook pancetta, turning frequently, in a skillet over medium-low heat until browned and crisp, 10 minutes. Drain on paper towels and cut into 1-inch wide strips. Pour off excess fat from skillet. Add butter and oil to skillet and melt over medium heat. Add scallions and cook, stirring constantly, until just soft, 2 minutes. Meanwhile, cook pasta in a large pot of boiling, salted water, until firm to the bite. Drain, reserving ½ cup pasta water. Add pasta with Parmesan and pancetta to scallions. Toss well to coat, adding reserved water as needed. Add salt and pepper to taste. Serve immediately with additional Parmesan.

WHICH PASTA?
Tubes or shapes—penne, rigatoni, gnocchi, conchiglie.

COOKS' NOTE
Try and match the size of the pasta to the size of your ingredients. Cut the pancetta into pieces that can be easily caught in the hollow of the pasta shape.

SAUSAGE WITH CREAM AND BASIL

SERVES 4

2 tbsp extra virgin olive oil
1 small onion, finely chopped
4 garlic cloves, crushed
8oz Italian sausages, casings
 removed and crumbled

1¼ cups heavy cream
1lb dried pasta
1 handful fresh basil leaves, torn
salt, black pepper
freshly grated Parmesan to serve

Heat oil in a skillet. Add onion and garlic and cook, stirring occasionally over medium-high heat, until just golden, 5 minutes. Add sausage and cook, stirring frequently to break up meat, until it just loses its pink color, 10 minutes. Stir in cream and simmer until just thickened, 1–2 minutes. Add salt and pepper to taste. Meanwhile, cook pasta in a large pot of boiling, salted water, until firm to the bite. Drain, reserving ½ cup pasta water. Add pasta with basil to the hot sauce. Toss well to coat, adding reserved water as needed. Serve immediately with Parmesan.

WHICH PASTA?
Shapes or tubes—conchiglie, fusilli, macaroni, penne, rigatoni.

PAN-ROASTED CHICKEN WITH GARLIC AND SHALLOTS

SERVES 4-6

4 boneless chicken breast halves
12 whole garlic cloves
8 whole shallots
¾ cup white wine
2 tbsp extra virgin olive oil
salt, black pepper
¾ cup heavy cream
1lb dried pasta

Preheat oven to 400°F.
Place chicken skin side up, with garlic and shallots, in a large ovenproof skillet. Add the wine. Drizzle chicken skin with oil and sprinkle with salt and pepper. Roast until chicken is cooked through and skin is crisp and golden, 25-30 minutes. Remove chicken, garlic, and shallots and cover to keep warm. Bring chicken juices to a simmer over medium-high heat. Add cream and cook, stirring constantly, until hot through, 1 minute. Add salt and pepper to taste. Meanwhile, cook pasta in a large pot of boiling, salted water, until firm to the bite. Drain. Add pasta to the hot sauce. Toss well to coat. Slice each chicken breast half crosswise into 3 pieces. Top pasta with chicken, garlic, and shallots. Serve immediately.

WHICH PASTA?
Medium to wide ribbons or large tubes—tagliatelle, pappardelle, penne, rigatoni.

COOKS' NOTE
Snipping off the tops of the roast garlic and shallots with kitchen scissors makes it easier to squeeze out the soft, sweet centers from their papery skins.

QUICK COOK
AMATRICIANA

SERVES 4

4 tbsp extra virgin olive oil
7oz unsmoked pancetta or
  bacon, cut into ¼-inch wide strips
½ tsp crushed red pepper flakes
6 tbsp dry white wine
1 onion, finely chopped
1 - 14oz can Italian plum tomatoes,
  chopped, or 1lb fresh tomatoes,
  peeled and chopped
salt, black pepper
1lb dried pasta
¼ cup freshly grated Pecorino
  Romano or Parmesan, plus
  additional cheese to serve

Heat oil in a skillet. Add pancetta strips
and red pepper flakes and cook, stirring
occasionally over medium heat, until
pancetta is crisp, 5 minutes. Add wine
and simmer until reduced by half,
1 minute. Add onion and cook, stirring
frequently, until soft and just golden,
10 minutes. Turn heat to medium high.
Add tomatoes and cook, until thickened,
10 minutes. Add salt and pepper to taste.
Meanwhile, cook pasta in a large pot of
boiling, salted water, until firm to the
bite. Drain. Add pasta with cheese to
the hot sauce. Toss well to coat. Serve
immediately with additional cheese.

WHICH PASTA?
Hollow strands or tubes—spaghetti, bucatini, penne,
rigatoni.

THINK AHEAD
Make sauce up to 1 day in advance. Cool completely.
Cover and refrigerate.

COOKS' NOTE
This sauce is made in the Apennines east of Rome
for the local Festa on August 15. The cheese used in
the traditional recipe is Pecorino Romano, which has
the right piquancy to match the flavor of the chili. If
you cannot find Pecorino Romano, you can use
Parmesan. The pancetta should be unsmoked.

QUICK COOK
CHICKEN WITH LEMON AND MUSHROOMS

SERVES 4

2 tbsp butter
2 skinless, boneless chicken breast halves, cut across into
 8 - 1-inch wide strips
2 garlic cloves, crushed
8oz cremini mushrooms, sliced
1 tsp fresh thyme leaves
2 tbsp lemon juice
salt, black pepper
1lb dried pasta
additional 2 tbsp butter to toss

Melt butter in a skillet over medium heat. Add chicken strips and cook, stirring
frequently, until opaque, 4 minutes. Add garlic, mushrooms, and thyme. Cook, stirring
frequently, until mushrooms are soft and chicken is cooked through, 4 minutes. Add
lemon juice and salt and pepper to taste. Meanwhile, cook pasta in a large pot of
boiling, salted water, until firm to the bite. Drain. Add pasta to hot sauce with 2 tbsp
additional butter. Toss well to coat. Serve immediately.

WHICH PASTA?
Medium to large ribbons—fettuccine, tagliatelle, pappardelle.

THINK AHEAD
Make sauce up to 1 day in advance. Cover and refrigerate. Reheat gently, adding 2 tbsp water.

QUICK COOK
CARBONARA

SERVES 4

3 egg yolks
½ cup freshly grated Parmesan
2 tbsp extra virgin olive oil
2 garlic cloves, peeled and halved
7oz unsmoked pancetta or
** bacon slices, cut into ¼-inch**
** wide strips**
¼ cup white wine
1 tbsp butter
1lb dried pasta
salt, black pepper
additional freshly grated Parmesan
** to serve**

Mix egg yolks and Parmesan in a bowl until combined. Heat oil in a skillet. Add garlic and cook over medium high heat until golden, 2 minutes. Remove garlic and discard. Add pancetta and cook, stirring occasionally, until crisp, 5 minutes. Add wine and simmer until just evaporated, 2 minutes. Remove from heat.
Meanwhile, cook pasta in a large pot of boiling, salted water, until firm to the bite. Drain, reserving ½ cup pasta water. Add drained pasta to the hot pancetta and toss well to coat. Remove from the heat. Add egg mixture and butter and toss again to coat, adding reserved water as needed. Add salt and pepper to taste. Serve immediately with additional Parmesan.

WHICH PASTA?
Hollow or thin strands—bucatini, spaghetti.

COOKS' NOTE
We have sharpened the sauce with the addition of white wine. If you don't have any white wine in the pantry, use 1 tbsp white wine vinegar or 2 tbsp dry vermouth instead.

QUICK COOK
VENETIAN-STYLE CHICKEN LIVER

SERVES 4

8oz chicken livers
2 tbsp butter
3 tbsp extra virgin olive oil
4 fresh sage leaves
1 garlic clove, peeled an halved
¼ cup dry white wine
salt, black pepper
1lb dried pasta
¼ cup freshly grated Parmesan
additional 1 tbsp butter to toss
additional freshly grated Parmesan to serve

Place chicken livers in strainer and rinse under cold running water. Drain and pat dry with paper towels. Cut each chicken liver into 3 pieces, discarding fat and membranes. Melt butter with olive oil in a skillet over medium heat. Add garlic and sage and cook until garlic is golden, 2–3 minutes. Remove and discard garlic and sage. Add chicken livers and cook, stirring frequently, until browned, 1 minute. Add wine and simmer until just evaporated, 30 seconds. Add salt and pepper to taste. Meanwhile, cook pasta in a large pot of boiling, salted water, until firm to the bite. Drain. Add pasta with Parmesan and 1 tbsp additional butter to the hot sauce. Toss well to coat. Serve immediately with additional Parmesan.

WHICH PASTA?
Shapes or medium to wide ribbons—conchiglie, pappardelle, tagliatelle, farfalle.

COOKS' NOTE
Quick cooking ensures that the chicken liver pieces will be still pink and juicy inside.

SLOW COOK
SPICY SAUSAGE RAGU

SERVES 4

3 tbsp extra virgin olive oil
1 onion, finely chopped
**2 garlic cloves, finely
   chopped**
**8oz Italian sausages, casings
   removed and crumbled**
½ tsp crushed red pepper flakes
1 tsp fennel seeds
1 tsp dried oregano
1 tbsp tomato paste
**1 - 14oz can chopped Italian
   plum tomatoes**
salt, black pepper
⅔ cup heavy cream
1lb dried pasta
freshly grated Parmesan to serve

Heat oil in a skillet. Cook onion and
garlic over medium high heat, stirring
frequently, until soft and pale gold,
5 minutes. Add sausage. Cook, stirring
to break up, until browned, 10 minutes.
Add red pepper flakes, fennel, oregano,
tomato paste, and chopped tomatoes.
Simmer, stirring occasionally, until
thickened, 20 minutes. Add cream. Cook,
stirring until heated through. Add salt
and pepper to taste.
Meanwhile, cook pasta in a large pot of
boiling, salted water, until firm to the
bite. Drain. Add pasta to the hot sauce.
Toss well to coat. Serve immediately
with Parmesan.

WHICH PASTA?
Medium or large tubes—cavatelli, penne,
rigatoni, macaroni.

THINK AHEAD
Make ragù up to 3 days in advance. Cover and
refrigerate. Alternatively, freeze up to 1 month in
advance. Defrost overnight in refrigerator
before reheating.

COOKS' NOTE
Be sure to use good-quality Italian sausage for this
sauce. You can use the sweet sausages or, for an
even spicier ragù, use spicy sausages.

SLOW COOK
CLASSIC RAGU BOLOGNESE

SERVES 4–6

4 tbsp (½ stick) butter
2 tbsp extra virgin olive oil
**2oz unsmoked pancetta or
   bacon, finely chopped**
1 small onion, finely chopped
1 carrot, finely chopped
1 celery stalk, finely chopped
1 garlic clove, finely chopped
1 bay leaf
1lb coarse-ground chuck

2 tbsp tomato paste
⅔ cup red wine
⅔ cup meat stock, or water
ground nutmeg
⅔ cup milk
salt, black pepper,
1lb dried pasta
freshly grated Parmesan to serve

Melt butter and oil in a large, heavy-bottomed pot over medium-high heat. Add
pancetta and cook, stirring frequently, until browned, 5 minutes. Add onion, carrot,
celery, garlic, and bay leaf and cook, stirring frequently, until soft, 8 minutes. Add
ground chuck and cook, crumbling with a fork to break up, until browned. Turn heat
to medium. Add tomato paste and cook, stirring constantly, 1 minute. Add wine,
stock, or water, and nutmeg. Bring to a boil, then turn heat down to very low.
Simmer, partially covered, stirring occasionally and adding milk 2 tbsp at a time every
20–30 minutes. Cook until thick and rich, 2 hours. Add salt and pepper to taste.
Cook pasta in a large pot of boiling, salted water until firm to the bite. Drain. Add
drained pasta to hot ragù. Toss well to coat. Serve immediately with Parmesan.

WHICH PASTA?
Medium ribbons or large tubes—tagliatelle, macaroni, rigatoni, penne.

THINK AHEAD
Make sauce up to 3 days in advance. Cover and refrigerate. Alternatively, make up to 1 month in advance and
freeze. Defrost overnight in refrigerator before reheating.

CHICKEN, TOMATO, AND ROSEMARY RAGU

SERVES 4

FOR CHICKEN

**12oz boneless, skinless
  chicken thighs
1 celery stalk, quartered
½ small onion, chopped
5 tbsp dry white wine**

FOR SAUCE

**5 tbsp extra virgin olive oil
1 tbsp finely chopped onion
1 tbsp finely chopped celery stalk
3 garlic cloves, finely chopped
1 tbsp finely chopped fresh
  flat-leaf parsley
1 tbsp finely chopped rosemary
grated zest of ½ lemon
1 - 14oz can Italian plum
  tomatoes, chopped
salt, black pepper
1lb dried pasta**

Place chicken, celery, onion, and wine
in a pan with cold water to cover. Bring
slowly to a simmer over medium low
heat. Simmer gently without boiling
until cooked through, 7–10 minutes.
Cool completely in cooking liquid.
Drain, reserving liquid, and cut chicken
into ½-inch dice.

To make the sauce, heat oil in a skillet.
Add onion and celery and cook, stirring
occasionally, over medium low heat until
soft, 5 minutes. Add garlic, parsley, and
rosemary and cook until fragrant,
1 minute. Add lemon zest, tomatoes, and
¼ cup reserved poaching liquid. Reduce
heat to low and simmer gently, stirring
occasionally, until thick, 30 minutes. Add
salt and pepper to taste. Add chicken
and heat through, 3 minutes. Meanwhile,
cook pasta in a large pot of boiling, salted
water, until firm to the bite. Drain. Add
pasta to the hot sauce. Toss well to coat.
Serve immediately.

WHICH PASTA?
Medium tubes or shapes—gnocchi,
cavatelli, macaroni.

THINK AHEAD
Cook chicken, but do not dice, up to 2 days in
advance. Make tomato sauce up to 1 day in
advance. Cover and refrigerate.

RAGU AL FORNO

SERVES 4-6
FOR BECHAMEL
**4 tbsp (½ stick) butter
3 tbsp all-purpose flour
2⅛ cups milk
salt, pepper, nutmeg**

**1lb dried pasta
1 recipe classic ragù bolognese (see
  page 91)
3 tbsp freshly grated Parmesan**

Preheat oven to 400°F.
For bechamel, melt butter over medium heat in a heavy saucepan. Whisk in flour
and cook until foaming, about 1 minute. Remove from heat and pour in milk
gradually, whisking constantly. Return to heat and cook, whisking constantly, until
sauce thickens, about 2 minutes. Bring to a boil and remove from heat. Add salt,
black pepper, and nutmeg to taste. Meanwhile, cook pasta in a large pot of boiling,
salted water, until just firm to the bite. Drain. Toss pasta with ragù, bechamel, and
Parmesan. Place in buttered 13 x 9 x 3-inch ovenproof dish and bake until golden
and crusty, 15 minutes. Let stand for 5 minutes before serving.

WHICH PASTA?
Large tubes or shapes—rigatoni, penne, conchiglie.

THINK AHEAD
Assemble and let cool completely. Cover, unbaked and refrigerate up to 1 day in advance. Alternatively, freeze
up to 3 weeks in advance. Defrost overnight in the refrigerator. Bake in preheated 400°F oven for 30 minutes
until golden and crusty. Let stand 5 minutes before serving.

SLOW COOK
CLASSIC LASAGNE AL FORNO

SERVES 6-8

**12 sheets dried or fresh lasagne, or 1 - 16oz package
lasagne noodles**
1 recipe classic ragù bolognese (see page 91)
6 tbsp freshly grated Parmesan

FOR BECHAMEL
5 tbsp butter
4½ tbsp all-purpose flour
3⅛ cups milk
salt, black pepper, nutmeg

Preheat oven to 400°F.

Cook pasta, 3 sheets, or noodles, at a time, in a large pot of
boiling, salted water for half the recommended time, or until
pasta is pliable but slightly hard at the center, about 4 minutes
for dried pasta, 1 minute for fresh pasta. Drain and place
sheets in a single layer on dish towels.

For bechamel, melt butter over medium heat in a heavy
saucepan. Whisk in flour and cook until foaming, about
1 minute. Remove from heat and pour in milk gradually,
whisking constantly. Return to heat and cook, whisking
constantly, until sauce thickens, about 2 minutes. Bring to a
boil and remove from the heat. Add salt, pepper, and nutmeg
to taste. In a buttered 13 x 9 x 3-inch ovenproof dish, spread
a thin layer of the bechamel. Lay one-quarter of the pasta
sheets, or noodles, over the bechamel. Spread a quarter of the
ragù over the pasta. Spread a quarter of the bechamel over the
ragù, and sprinkle with a quarter of the Parmesan. Starting
with another quarter of the sheets, or noodles, repeat layers.
Repeat layers again to finish, ending with Parmesan. Bake in
oven until golden and bubbling, 30 minutes. Let stand for
5 minutes before serving.

WHICH PASTA?
Egg lasagne, green or yellow, fresh when possible.

THINK AHEAD
Assemble lasagne and let cool completely. Cover, unbaked, and refrigerate up to
1 day in advance. Alternatively freeze, unbaked, up to 3 weeks in advance.
Defrost overnight in refrigerator. Cook in preheated 400°F oven for 30 minutes.
Make bechamel up to 2 days in advance. Cover with plastic wrap, pressing down
on the surface to prevent a skin from forming. Refrigerate. Before using, beat to
make it easy to spread. If making with cold bechamel, be sure to have ragù and
pasta also cold.

COOKS' NOTE
We don't recommend no-cook lasagne, but if it is all you can find at the store,
always treat it as regular dried lasagne and precook until just pliable, about 30
seconds. Alternatively, follow the lasagne recipe on the package, which will make
the allowances for the amount of liquid absorbed by the lasagne during baking.

VARIATION
CLASSIC ITALIAN-AMERICAN LASAGNE
Omit bechamel. Use 1 cup ricotta, and 8oz finely sliced
mozzarella in place of bechamel. Arrange in layers as directed,
substituting ricotta and mozzarella mixture for bechamel. Bake
as directed.

Puglie

A deliciously fruity filtered
Ogliarola and Barese olives

EXCLUSIVELY IMP

PASTA WITH OLIVES
AND OLIVE OIL

OLIVE OIL IN THE PASTA PANTRY

Always use olive oil when cooking pasta sauces.

We buy extra virgin olive oil, which is made from the first pressing of the olives. It may cost a little more, but its superior quality makes it worth the extra expense. The relative cost of good extra virgin olive oil is not excessive when compared to a bottle of fine wine, which is finished at one sitting.

However, there is no need to use the best quality olive oil for everything. It is a good idea to have at least 2 bottles open at the same time. You can use a lighter, less costly oil for cooking and keep a superior one for seasoning and drizzling. Although both oils should be extra virgin, there's no need to buy anything but the least expensive available to use for cooking. Your choice of oil for drizzling and tossing only is entirely personal. It shouldn't necessarily be Italian; we suggest that you try out a few, from different regions in Italy, as well as from different countries, until you find one you like.

The color of olive oil has to do with the timing of the harvest—the very dark green olive oil is from an early harvest, while later harvests yield golden oil—but this is not in itself an indication of quality. Unlike wine, olive oil does not improve with age. It is best stored in a cool, dark place at around 50–60°F and should not be kept for longer than 1 year, after which many oils will start to taste stale.

Green and black olives are not interchangeable. Their taste and texture are different. Black olives owe their dark, rich flavor to being harvested when fully ripe. Green olives are picked before they are ripe and have a firm texture and a tangy taste. Olives are best bought loose and in small quantities since they will spoil within a few days unless generously covered with olive oil. Always have a few jars or cans of good quality olives on hand as a standby.

98

NO COOK
OLIVE OIL

SERVES 4

1lb dried pasta
½ cup extra virgin olive oil
salt, crushed red pepper flakes

Cook pasta in a large pot of boiling, salted water, until firm to the bite. Drain, reserving ½ cup pasta water. Toss pasta with oil, adding reserved water as needed. Add salt and red pepper flakes to taste.

WHICH PASTA?
Strands—spaghettini, spaghetti.

COOKS' NOTE
We like to use a rich peppery Tuscan or Umbrian olive oil for this recipe, where the flavor of the olive oil is so important.

VARIATIONS

LEMON OLIVE OIL
Add ½ tsp grated lemon zest and 2 tbsp fresh lemon juice with the olive oil to pasta.

GARLIC OLIVE OIL
Add 2 crushed garlic cloves with the olive oil to pasta.

FRESH HERB OLIVE OIL
Add 1 handful of fresh flat-leaf parsley or basil, chopped, with the olive oil, to the pasta.

NO COOK
CHILI OLIVE PESTO

SERVES 4

¾ **cup pitted black olives, such as**
  kalamata or gaeta, or green olives
1 garlic clove, crushed
½ **tsp crushed red pepper flakes**
6 tbsp extra virgin olive oil
1lb dried pasta
salt, black pepper

Place olives, garlic, red pepper flakes, and oil in a food processor or blender; pulse until blended but still retaining some texture.

Cook pasta in a large pot of boiling, salted water, until firm to the bite if serving hot. If serving this dish as a salad, slightly undercook the pasta. Drain, reserving ½ cup pasta water. Return pasta with pesto to the warm pasta pot. Toss well to coat, adding reserved water as needed. Add salt and pepper to taste. Serve immediately or at room temperature.

WHICH PASTA?
Strands or thin ribbons—spaghetti, spaghettini, linguine.

NO COOK
OLIVE, ANCHOVY, AND CAPER PESTO

SERVES 4

1 cup pitted black olives, such as
  kalamata or gaeta
4 anchovy fillets, drained
2 tbsp drained capers, rinsed
1 garlic clove, crushed
¼ **tsp dried thyme**
6 tbsp olive oil
1lb dried pasta

Place olives, anchovies, capers, garlic, thyme, and oil in a food processor or blender; pulse to a paste. Cook pasta in a large pot of boiling, salted water, until firm to the bite if serving hot. If serving this dish as a salad, slightly undercook the pasta. Drain, reserving ½ cup pasta water. Return pasta with pesto to the warm pasta pot. Toss well to coat, adding reserved water as needed. Serve immediately or at room temperature.

WHICH PASTA?
Small shapes—pennette, conchiglie, fusilli.

THINK AHEAD
Make pestos up to 4 days in advance. Cover and refrigerate. If serving as a salad, dress up to 8 hours in advance. Cover and store at room temperature.

QUICK COOK
SPICY LEMON OLIVE

SERVES 4

6 tbsp extra virgin olive oil
1lb dried pasta
2 - ½ -inch-wide strips of thin
 lemon rind
1 - 2oz-can anchovy fillets,
 drained and chopped
15 pitted black olives, such as
 kalamata or gaeta, sliced
2 cloves garlic, finely chopped
½ tsp crushed red pepper flakes
salt, black pepper
¼ cup chopped fresh flat-leaf parsley
freshly grated Pecorino Romano
 to serve

Cook pasta in a large pot of boiling,
salted water, until firm to the bite.
While pasta is cooking, heat oil in a
skillet. Add lemon rind and cook over
low heat until sizzling, 2 minutes. Add
anchovies and cook, stirring constantly,
until disintegrated, 2–3 minutes. Add
olives, garlic, and red pepper flakes.
Cook until fragrant, 2 minutes. Add salt
and pepper to taste. Remove and discard
lemon rind. Drain pasta, reserving
½ cup pasta water. Add pasta with
parsley to the hot sauce. Toss well to
coat, adding reserved water as needed.
Serve immediately with Pecorino.

WHICH PASTA?
Shapes or shells—fusilli, conchiglie, farfalle.

COOKS' NOTE
Preserved anchovy fillets must be cooked over
a gentle heat or they will become bitter. We
recommend either Tuscan or Pugliese olive oil
in this recipe.

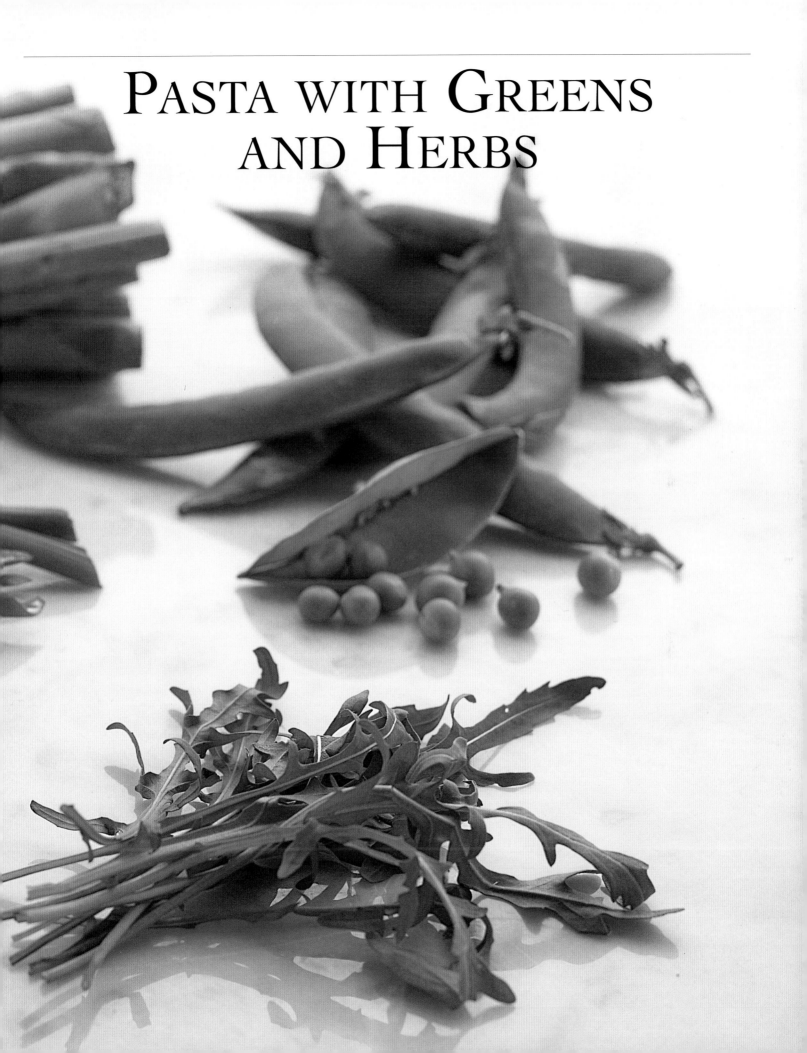

PASTA WITH GREENS AND HERBS

GREENS AND HERBS IN THE PASTA PANTRY

When buying fresh herbs, choose as you would fresh flowers. They should be vibrant green and bursting with life. The less fresh the herb, the less flavor it has. Fresh parsley and basil are the most essential fresh herbs in the pasta pantry, and dried just will not do as an alternative.

We prefer Italian flat-leaf parsley, because it is more aromatic than the curly variety. Chopped parsley freezes well; store in an airtight container and scoop out a tablespoon or so as needed. Basil is best torn rather than chopped, since chopping damages its delicate flavor and color.

Bunches of fresh herbs can be stored in the refrigerator, either in a glass of water with a plastic bag placed loosely over them, or in a plastic tub with their stalks removed. Choose greens that are firm, crisp, and fresh looking. Cauliflower and broccoli should have juicy-looking stalks that show no signs of discoloring. Choose bright-looking zucchini that are very firm. When buying fresh peas, look for bright, snappy pods. Frozen peas are a perfectly acceptable substitute for fresh; in fact they are highly preferable to anything but locally grown new-season peas in the pod.

NO COOK
SIMPLE BASIL PESTO

SERVES 4

1½ cups fresh basil leaves
2 garlic cloves
2 tbsp pine nuts
½ cup extra virgin olive oil
½ cup freshly grated Parmesan
salt

1lb dried pasta

Place basil, garlic, pine nuts, and olive oil in a food processor; pulse until smooth. Transfer to a bowl. Stir in Parmesan until well combined. Salt to taste. Set aside or store, see below. Cook pasta in a large pot of boiling, salted water, until firm to the bite if serving hot. If serving this dish as a salad, slightly undercook pasta. Drain, reserving ½ cup pasta water. Return pasta with the pesto to the warm pasta pot. Toss well to coat, adding reserved water as needed. Serve immediately or at room temperature.

WHICH PASTA?
Thin ribbons or strands—trenette, linguine, spaghetti, spaghettini.

THINK AHEAD
Make pesto up to 4 days in advance. Cover and refrigerate. Alternatively, make pesto without Parmesan and freeze for up to 3 months. Add Parmesan and seasoning when defrosted. If serving as a salad, dress pasta up to 8 hours in advance. Cover and store at room temperature.

COOKS' NOTE
Traditionally pesto is only made with a sweet-flavored olive oil such as one from Liguria.

VARIATIONS

BEST BASIL PESTO
Make pesto as directed reducing olive oil to 5 tbsp. Add 3 tbsp softened butter to the basil mixture with the Parmesan.

BASIL PESTO CREAM
Make pesto as directed, adding 3 tbsp sour cream, crème fraîche, or plain yogurt to the basil mixture with the Parmesan.

BASIL RICOTTA PESTO
Make pesto as directed, adding 3 tbsp ricotta to the basil mixture with the Parmesan.

NO-COOK
EVEN SIMPLER BASIL PESTO

SERVES 4

1lb dried pasta
1½ cups fresh basil leaves, torn
2 tbsp pine nuts, toasted (see page 160)
2 garlic cloves, crushed
6 tbsp freshly grated Parmesan
½ cup extra virgin olive oil
salt

Cook pasta in a large pot of boiling, salted water, until just firm to the bite. Drain, reserving ½ cup pasta water. Return pasta with basil, pine nuts, garlic, Parmesan, and oil to the warm pasta pot. Toss well to coat, adding reserved water as needed. Add salt to taste. Serve immediately.

WHICH PASTA?
Shapes or tubes—conchiglie, penne, cavatelli.

NO COOK
SPINACH AND WALNUT PESTO

SERVES 4

1 cup packed, stemmed spinach leaves
4 garlic cloves, crushed
3 tbsp walnut pieces
6 tbsp extra virgin olive oil
½ cup freshly grated Parmesan
salt, black pepper
1lb dried pasta

Place spinach, garlic, walnuts, and olive oil in a food processor
or blender; pulse until smooth. Transfer to a bowl. Mix in
Parmesan until well combined. Add salt and pepper to taste.
Set aside or store, see below.
Cook pasta in a large pot of boiling, salted water until firm to
the bite if serving hot. If serving this dish as a salad, slightly
undercook pasta. Drain, reserving ½ cup pasta water. Return
pasta with pesto to the pot. Toss well to coat, adding reserved
water as needed. Serve immediately or at room temperature.

WHICH PASTA?
Large pasta tubes or shells—rigatoni, gnocchetti rigati, conchiglie.

THINK AHEAD
Make pesto up to 4 days in advance. Cover and refrigerate. Alternatively, make
pesto without cheese and freeze for up to 3 months. Add cheese and seasoning
when defrosted. If serving as a salad, dress pasta up to 8 hours in advance. Cover
and store at room temperature.

VARIATION
PARSLEY PESTO
Replace spinach with ¾ cup fresh flat-leaf parsley. Make
as directed.

QUICK COOK
FRAGRANT FRESH HERB

SERVES 4

1lb dried pasta
½ cup extra virgin
olive oil
1 garlic clove, finely
chopped
1 handful fresh flat-leaf
parsley, finely chopped

2 tbsp finely chopped fresh
oregano, marjoram,
or basil
½ tbsp finely chopped fresh
rosemary, thyme, or sage
salt, black pepper

Cook pasta in a large pot of boiling, salted water, until firm to
the bite. While pasta is cooking, heat oil in a skillet. Add garlic
and herbs, and cook over medium heat until fragrant, 1 minute.
Add salt and pepper to taste. Drain pasta, reserving ½ cup pasta
water. Add pasta to the hot sauce. Toss well to coat, adding
reserved water as needed. Serve immediately.

WHICH PASTA?
Thin ribbons—linguine, spaghettini.

COOKS' NOTE
You can vary the kind of herbs, depending on what you have in the garden or you
find in the store, but parsley must always be included.

SIZZLING SAGE BUTTER

SERVES 4

1lb dried pasta
6 tbsp butter
2 garlic cloves, peeled and halved
16 fresh sage leaves
freshly grated Parmesan to serve

Cook pasta in a large pot of boiling, salted water, until firm to the bite. While pasta is cooking, heat butter and garlic in a skillet over a medium heat until just golden. Add sage leaves and cook, stirring, until fragrant, 30 seconds. Remove and discard garlic. Drain pasta and return to the warm pasta pot. Add hot butter and sage to pasta. Toss well to coat. Serve immediately with plenty of Parmesan.

WHICH PASTA?
Medium ribbons or stuffed pasta—fettuccine, tagliatelle, ravioli, tortellini, cappelletti.

FRESH HERBS AND GOLDEN CRUMBS

SERVES 4

1lb dried pasta
5 tbsp extra virgin olive oil
¾ cup fresh breadcrumbs
4 scallions, finely chopped
1 handful fresh parsley, basil, oregano, or a combination, coarsely chopped
additional extra virgin olive oil
salt, black pepper

Cook pasta in a large pot of boiling, salted water, until firm to the bite. While pasta is cooking, heat oil in a skillet. Add breadcrumbs and cook, stirring constantly over medium high heat, until crisp and golden, 5–8 minutes. Add scallions and your choice of herbs and stir to combine. Drain pasta. Add drained pasta to the crumbs with 2 tbsp additional oil. Toss to coat. Add salt and pepper to taste. Serve immediately.

WHICH PASTA?
Strands or shapes—spaghetti, conchiglie, fusilli.

ZUCCHINI AND BASIL WITH CREAM

SERVES 4

2 tbsp butter
2 tbsp extra virgin olive oil
1lb small zucchini, cut into
 ¼-inch thick slices
4 garlic cloves, finely chopped
1¼ cups heavy cream
1 handful torn fresh basil leaves
salt, black pepper
1lb dried pasta
¼ cup freshly grated Parmesan, plus
 additional to serve

Melt butter with olive oil in a skillet. Add zucchini and garlic and cook, stirring frequently over medium heat, until just golden, 5–10 minutes. Reduce heat to medium low. Add cream and simmer gently until just thickened, 2 minutes. Add basil with salt and pepper to taste. Meanwhile, cook pasta in a large pot of boiling, salted water, until firm to the bite. Drain. Add pasta with Parmesan to the hot sauce. Toss well to coat. Serve immediately with additional Parmesan.

WHICH PASTA?
Tubes or shapes—farfalle, penne, cavatelli.

VARIATION
ZUCCHINI WITH HAM
Add 4 ham slices cut into short, fine strips, 1 inch long and ¼ inch wide, to the zucchini with the garlic. Finish as directed.

PEAS, PROSCIUTTO, AND FRESH HERBS

SERVES 4

1lb fresh peas (unshelled weight) or 2 cups tiny frozen peas, defrosted
6 tbsp butter
4oz prosciutto slices, cut into short, fine strips, about 1 inch long
 and ¼ inch wide
salt, black pepper
1lb dried pasta
6 tbsp freshly grated Parmesan
2 tbsp finely chopped fresh mint, basil, or flat-leaf parsley, optional
additional freshly grated Parmesan to serve

If using fresh peas, cook in boiling salted water until just tender, 5–8 minutes. Drain. Cook pasta in a large pot of boiling, salted water, until firm to the bite. While pasta is cooking, melt butter in a skillet. Add peas and prosciutto and cook, stirring constantly over medium heat, until hot through, 2 minutes. Add salt and pepper to taste. Drain pasta, reserving ½ cup pasta water. Add pasta with Parmesan and your chosen herb, if using, to the hot sauce. Toss well to coat, adding reserved water as needed. Serve immediately with additional Parmesan.

WHICH PASTA?
Medium to wide ribbons—fettuccine, tagliatelle, pappardelle.

VARIATION
ASPARAGUS, PROSCIUTTO, AND FRESH HERBS
Omit peas. Cook 3 cups small asparagus tips in boiling salted water until just tender, 2–3 minutes. Finish as directed.

SPICY BROCCOLI WITH GOLDEN GARLIC

SERVES 4

**1lb broccoli, stalks chopped
and head separated into florets
½ cup extra virgin olive oil
4 garlic cloves, finely sliced
½ tsp crushed red pepper flakes
salt, black pepper
1lb dried pasta**

Cook broccoli in a pan of boiling, salted water until just tender, 3–5 minutes. Heat oil in a skillet. Add garlic and cook over medium high heat until just golden, 2 minutes. Add drained broccoli and red pepper flakes and cook, stirring occasionally, for 5 minutes. Add salt and pepper to taste. Meanwhile, cook pasta in a large pot of boiling, salted water until firm to the bite. Drain. Add pasta to the hot sauce. Toss well to coat. Serve immediately.

WHICH PASTA?
Shapes—orecchiette, gnocchi, conchiglie.

COOKS' NOTE
We like to use a peppery olive oil from Puglia or Tuscany in this recipe to complement the spicy red pepper flakes.

VARIATIONS

SPICY BROCCOLI WITH GOLDEN GARLIC AND ANCHOVIES

Add 4 drained, chopped anchovies to the oil with the garlic. Finish as directed.

SPICY CAULIFLOWER WITH GOLDEN GARLIC

Omit broccoli. Cook 1lb cauliflower florets in boiling, salted water until just tender, 5–7 minutes. Drain. Finish sauce as directed.

SPICY BROCCOLI RABE WITH GOLDEN GARLIC

Omit broccoli. Replace with 1lb coarsely chopped broccoli rabe. Finish sauce as directed.

ASPARAGUS WITH CREAM

SERVES 4

**1lb asparagus, cut into 1-inch pieces, using only tips
and tender parts of stem
1lb dried pasta
5 tbsp unsalted butter
2 tbsp finely chopped onion
⅔ cup heavy cream
nutmeg, salt, black pepper
2 tbsp freshly grated Parmesan, plus additional to serve**

Cook asparagus in a pan of boiling, salted water until just tender, 3–5 minutes. Drain and plunge into cold water to cool completely. Drain and reserve. Cook pasta in a large pot of boiling, salted water, until firm to the bite. While pasta is cooking, melt butter in a skillet. Add onion and cook, stirring occasionally over medium heat, until soft, 5 minutes. Add asparagus and cream and simmer gently until the cream is just thickened, 1–2 minutes. Add nutmeg, salt, and pepper to taste. Drain pasta, reserving ½ cup pasta water. Add drained pasta with Parmesan to the hot sauce. Toss gently, being careful not to break up asparagus tips and adding reserved water as needed. Serve immediately with additional Parmesan.

WHICH PASTA?
Medium tubes or ribbons—cavatelli, macaroni, fettuccine, tagliatelle.

SHREDDED ZUCCHINI WITH GOLDEN GARLIC

SERVES 4

1lb dried pasta
6 tbsp extra virgin olive oil
4–6 garlic cloves, finely sliced
4 small zucchini, grated
salt, black pepper
8 tbsp freshly grated Parmesan, plus additional to serve

Cook pasta in a large pot of boiling, salted water, until firm to the bite. While pasta is cooking, heat oil in a skillet. Add garlic and cook over high heat until just golden, 2 minutes. Add zucchini and cook, stirring constantly, until soft, 5 minutes. Remove cooked zucchini and garlic mixure from skillet and place into a colander. Press out excess liquid. Return zucchini to the skillet and add salt and pepper to taste. Drain pasta, reserving ½ cup pasta water. Add drained pasta with Parmesan to the hot zucchini. Toss well to coat, adding reserved water as needed. Serve immediately with additional Parmesan.

WHICH PASTA?

Medium shapes or ribbons—gnocchi, conchiglie, orecchiette, linguine, fettuccine, tagliatelle.

VARIATIONS

WILTED SPINACH WITH GOLDEN GARLIC

Omit zucchini. Use 1lb spinach, stemmed and roughly chopped. Cook garlic as directed. Add spinach and cook, stirring constantly, until soft, 2 minutes. Finish as directed.

WILTED LEEKS WITH GOLDEN GARLIC

Omit zucchini. Use 3 medium leeks, halved lengthwise and finely sliced. Cook garlic as directed. Add leeks and cook, stirring constantly, until wilted, 5 minutes. Cover and cook, stirring occasionally, until soft, 10 minutes. Finish as directed.

QUICK COOK
PRIMAVERA

SERVES 4

4 tbsp (½ stick) butter
2 tbsp extra virgin olive oil
1 tbsp finely chopped onion
1 small garlic clove, finely chopped
1 medium carrot, diced
1 medium celery stalk, diced
1 small zucchini, diced
1 cup green beans, cut into ½-inch pieces
1½ cups asparagus, tips cut into 1-inch lengths
**   and tender parts of stem cut into ½-inch pieces**
2 cups tiny frozen peas, defrosted, or 8oz
**   (unshelled weight) fresh peas, shelled**
¾ –1 cup chicken or vegetable stock
salt, black pepper
freshly grated Parmesan to serve

Melt butter with oil in a skillet over medium low heat. Add onion and cook, stirring constantly, until just soft, 3 minutes. Add garlic, carrot, celery, zucchini, green beans, asparagus, and peas and cook, stirring frequently, until almost tender, 10 minutes. Add stock just to cover and simmer gently until the liquid has almost evaporated and the vegetables are soft, 10 minutes. Add salt and pepper to taste. Meanwhile, cook pasta in a large pot of boiling, salted water, until firm to the bite. Drain. Add drained pasta to the hot sauce. Toss well to coat. Serve immediately with Parmesan.

WHICH PASTA?
Strands, thin ribbons or shapes—spaghetti, linguine, farfalle, gnocchi, conchiglie.

THINK AHEAD
Make sauce up to 1 day in advance. Cool completely. Cover and refrigerate. Reheat slowly over low heat, stirring gently.

VARIATIONS
PRIMAVERA WITH CREAM

Make sauce as directed using only 3 tbsp butter. Stir in ½ cup heavy cream to finished sauce. Simmer gently until just thickened, 2 minutes. Serve as directed.

PRIMAVERA PESTO

Make sauce as directed. Add 4 tbsp simple basil pesto (see page 105) or store-bought basil pesto, with the drained pasta, to the hot sauce. Serve as directed.

SLOW COOK
SPINACH AND RICOTTA LASAGNE

SERVES 4

12 sheets dried or fresh lasagne, or 1 - 16oz package lasagne noodles
2lbs spinach, washed
1 cup ricotta
2 tbsp butter, melted
salt, black pepper, nutmeg
8 tbsp freshly grated Parmesan

FOR BECHAMEL
5 tbsp butter
4½ tbsp all-purpose flour
3⅛ cups milk
salt, black pepper, nutmeg

Preheat oven to 350°F

Cook pasta, 3 sheets or noodles at a time, in a large pot of boiling, salted water for half the time recommended on the package, or until pasta is pliable but slightly hard at the center, 4 minutes for dried pasta, 1 minute for fresh pasta. Drain and place sheets in a single layer on dish towels.

Place wet spinach in a dry pan. Cover pan and place over medium heat and cook until tender, stirring frequently, about 5 minutes. Drain and, as soon as it is cool enough to handle, squeeze dry with your hands and coarsely chop. Combine spinach, ricotta, and butter. Add salt, pepper, and nutmeg to taste. Set aside.

For bechamel, melt butter over medium heat in a heavy sauce-pan. Whisk in flour and cook until foaming, about 1 minute. Remove from heat and pour in milk gradually, whisking constantly. Return to heat and cook, whisking constantly, until sauce thickens, about 2 minutes. Bring to a boil and remove from heat. Add salt, pepper, and nutmeg to taste.

Pour a thin layer of the bechamel just to cover the bottom of a 13 x 9 x 3-inch buttered ovenproof dish. Lay one quarter of the pasta sheets, or noodles, over the bechamel. Spread a quarter of the spinach-ricotta mixture over the pasta. Pour over one quarter of the bechamel and sprinkle a quarter of the Parmesan on top. Starting with another quarter of pasta sheets, or noodles, repeat layers. Repeat layers again to finish, ending with Parmesan. Bake until golden and bubbling, 20–30 minutes. Let stand for 5 minutes before serving.

WHICH PASTA?
Egg lasagne, fresh where possible.

COOKS' NOTE
We don't recommend no-cook lasagne, but if it is all you can find at the store, treat it as regular dried lasagne for this recipe and precook until just pliable, about 30 seconds.

THINK AHEAD
Assemble lasagne and leave to cool completely. Cover, unbaked, and refrigerate up to 1 day in advance. Alternatively freeze, unbaked, up to 3 weeks in advance. Defrost overnight in refrigerator. Cook in preheated 400°F oven for 30 minutes.

Make bechamel up to 2 days in advance. Cover with plastic wrap, pressing down on the surface to prevent a skin from forming. Refrigerate. Before using, return to room temperature and beat to make it easy to spread.

OTHER VEGETARIAN LASAGNES
SPINACH, GORGONZOLA, AND PINE NUT LASAGNE

Have ready 1½ cups crumbled Gorgonzola and ¼ cup pine nuts. Assemble lasagne as directed, covering each layer of spinach-ricotta mixture with one quarter Gorgonzola and 1 tbsp pine nuts before covering with bechamel and Parmesan. Finish as directed.

EGGPLANT, BASIL, AND MOZZARELLA LASAGNE

Omit spinach. Have ready 9½ cups of ½-inch dice eggplant, 2 cups grated mozzarella, and 1 handful torn fresh basil. Spread eggplant pieces out in a roasting pan and drizzle with 3 tbsp extra virgin olive oil. Roast in a preheated 400°F oven until soft, 20 minutes. Add salt and pepper to taste. Assemble lasagne as directed, covering each layer of pasta with one quarter ricotta, one quarter eggplant dice, one quarter grated mozzarella, and one quarter torn basil before covering with bechamel and Parmesan. Finish as directed.

MUSHROOM, GARLIC, AND PARSLEY LASAGNE

Omit spinach. Have ready 1½lbs (about 10 cups) sliced cremini or wild mushrooms, 2 tbsp extra virgin olive oil, 3 finely chopped garlic cloves, and 1 handful finely chopped fresh flat-leaf parsley. Heat oil in skillet. Add mushrooms and garlic and cook, stirring constantly, over medium high heat until just browned, 5 minutes. Add parsley and remove from heat. Add salt and pepper to taste. Assemble lasagne as directed, covering each layer of pasta with one quarter ricotta and one quarter mushroom mixture before covering with bechamel and Parmesan. Finish as directed.

PASTA WITH BEANS AND LENTILS

BEANS AND LENTILS IN THE PASTA PANTRY

Although dried, all legumes should still have a fresh, unwrinkled look. Dried beans, chickpeas, and lentils should be eaten within 12 months of being harvested, so renew your pantry supply yearly. If kept any longer they can become too dry and not cook properly until tender, however long you soak or boil them.

Chickpeas need soaking at least overnight and can take up to 4 hours to cook until tender. Luckily, canned chickpeas are a perfectly good substitute for dried, if well rinsed before using. If you can take the time, chickpeas taste nicer if they are skinned first. Place the cooked chickpeas in a bowl and cover with water. Gently rub the chickpeas between your fingers. The skins will slip off and float, while the chickpeas will sink. When you have finished, pour off the water and the skins together.

Lentils are an excellent pantry basic, since you don't have to soak them before cooking. For a truly Italian flavor, choose the small, brown Umbrian lentils which keep their shape when cooked. The very best are labeled Castelluccio; seek them out in good supermarkets and gourmet or Italian stores. Gray-green French puy lentils are a good substitute since they also hold their shape well when cooked.

Fresh green beans should be firm and bright-looking. Look for green beans that are bright and snap readily when bent. Avoid dull or limp beans. Buy fresh fava beans in the pod; choose smooth pods without wrinkled skins or blackened ends. The fava bean season is short, but small frozen beans are a good substitute. Unless very fresh and tender, fava beans are best skinned. Plunge into boiling water for 1 minute to loosen skins. Cool in cold water before draining and peeling.

CHICKPEAS WITH ROSEMARY, CHILI, AND GARLIC

SERVES 4

1lb dried pasta
6 tbsp extra virgin olive oil
4 garlic cloves, finely chopped
½ tsp crushed red pepper flakes
2 tsp finely chopped fresh rosemary or
  1 tsp dried rosemary, crumbled
1- 14oz can chickpeas, drained and rinsed
2 tbsp finely chopped fresh flat-leaf parsley
additional extra virgin olive oil
salt, black pepper

Cook pasta in a large pot of boiling, salted water, until firm to the bite. While pasta is cooking, heat oil in a skillet. Add garlic, red pepper flakes, and rosemary and cook over medium-high heat until fragrant, 1 minute. Add chickpeas and cook until sizzling hot, 3 minutes. Drain pasta, reserving ½ cup pasta water. Add pasta with parsley to the hot sauce. Toss well to coat, adding 2 tbsp additional olive oil, salt, pepper, and reserved water as needed. Serve immediately.

WHICH PASTA?
Large tubes or shells—conchiglie, rigatoni, penne.

VARIATION
FAVA BEANS WITH PECORINO
Cook just 2 garlic cloves with chili as directed. Omit rosemary and chickpeas. Replace with 1lb frozen fava beans, defrosted and cooked with 3 tbsp water until beans are tender and water has evaporated, 3–5 minutes. Add drained pasta with 4 tbsp freshly grated Pecorino to hot sauce. Finish as directed.

BRAISED UMBRIAN LENTILS

SERVES 4–6

1½ cups Umbrian or
 Puy lentils
1 medium onion, cut in half
6 fresh sage leaves
2 fresh rosemary sprigs
1 tbsp salt
1 lb dried pasta
4 medium-sized fresh ripe tomatoes,
 peeled, seeded, (see page 156) and
 chopped or 4 canned Italian plum
 tomatoes, chopped
2 garlic cloves, finely chopped
1 handful fresh flat-leaf
 parsley, chopped
5 tbsp extra virgin olive oil, plus
 additional for serving
freshly grated Pecorino Romano
 or Parmesan

Place lentils, onion, sage, rosemary, and
salt in a large heavy-bottomed pot.
Cover with 3 quarts cold water. Bring to
a boil over medium-high heat, stirring
occasionally. Simmer gently until tender,
15–20 minutes. Bring water to a boil.
Add pasta to pot and cook until pasta is
just firm to the bite.
Place tomatoes, garlic, parsley, and oil in
a skillet over medium low heat. Cook
3–4 minutes until tomatoes soften. When
pasta is just firm to the bite, use a slotted
spoon to transfer pasta and lentils to the
skillet, removing and discarding onion
pieces and herbs. Turn heat to medium
high and cook, stirring constantly,
2–3 minutes. Serve immediately, with
2 tbsp additional olive oil and Pecorino
Romano or Parmesan.

WHICH PASTA?
Shapes—conchiglie, gnocchi.

COOKS' NOTE
It is worth trying to find small, brown Umbrian
lentils (see page 122). They give this dish an
authentic flavor and texture.

CLASSIC GENOESE PESTO

SERVES 4

⅛ lb haricot verts (French baby
 green beans)
4 small new potatoes, sliced ⅛ in thick
1 lb dried pasta
1 recipe simple basil pesto
 (see page 105)
3 tbsp extra virgin olive oil
salt

Cook haricot verts in a large pot of
boiling salted water until tender, about
5 minutes. Remove with a slotted spoon.
Cool completely, by plunging into cold
water, and reserve. Add potatoes to the
pot and cook until tender in the center
when pierced with the tip of a small,
sharp knife, 6–8 minutes. Remove with a
slotted spoon and reserve. Add pasta to
the pot and cook until firm to the bite if
serving hot. If serving this dish as a
salad, slightly undercook pasta. Return
beans and potatoes to pot just before
draining pasta, to heat through, 1 minute.
Drain pasta, beans, and potatoes,
reserving ½ cup water. Return pasta,
beans, and potatoes with the pesto and
olive oil to the warm pasta pot. Toss
well, adding reserved water as needed.
Add salt to taste. Serve immediately or
at room temperature.

WHICH PASTA?
Strands or thin ribbons—linguine, trenette, spaghetti.

THINK AHEAD
Cook beans and potatoes up to 1 day in advance.
Cool completely. Cover.
If serving as a salad, dress pasta up to 8 hours in
advance. Cover and store at room temperature.

Pasta with Garlic

GARLIC IN THE PASTA PANTRY

When choosing garlic, look for firm, plump bulbs. Cloves that are shriveled will be dry with a musty, slightly metallic taste. Before chopping, we advise cutting garlic cloves in half and removing the inner green stem, since it has a slightly bitter flavor. New-season fresh garlic is sweet and tender and can be used liberally.

For only a hint of garlic flavor, peel a clove of garlic, cut in half and cook in the butter or oil, removing and discarding when golden. Some cooks put a wooden toothpick through the garlic clove so it can be spotted easily and removed whenever it has released enough flavor.

When frying garlic, be careful not to let it burn because it will give a bitter taste to the sauce.

Store garlic in a cool, dark place. The simplest way to peel garlic is to crush it with the flat side of a large knife (see page 156).

QUICK COOK
OLIO AGLIO

SERVES 4
1lb dried pasta
½ cup extra virgin olive oil
4 garlic cloves, finely chopped
salt, black pepper

Cook pasta in a large pot of boiling, salted water, until firm to the bite. While pasta is cooking, heat oil in a skillet. Add garlic and cook, stirring occasionally, over medium heat until golden, 2 minutes. Add salt and pepper to taste. Drain pasta. Add drained pasta to oil and garlic in the pan. Toss well to coat. Serve immediately.

WHICH PASTA?
Strands—spaghetti, spaghettini.

VARIATIONS
OLIO AGLIO PEPERONCINO
Add ½ tsp crushed red pepper flakes with garlic. Finish as directed.

OLIVE OIL, GARLIC, AND PARSLEY
Add 3 tbsp chopped fresh flat-leaf parsley with garlic. Finish as directed.

OLIVE OIL, GARLIC, AND FRESH TOMATO
Add 3 ripe fresh tomatoes, peeled, seeded (see page 156), and chopped with garlic. Finish as directed.

ROASTED GARLIC AND CHERRY TOMATOES

SERVES 4

2lbs cherry tomatoes, halved
16 garlic cloves, peeled
½ cup extra virgin olive oil
¼ tsp crushed red pepper flakes
½ tsp salt
¼ tsp black pepper
1lb dried pasta
1 handful torn fresh basil leaves

Preheat oven to 400°F.
Arrange tomatoes and garlic cloves so that they fit snugly in an oven tray or ovenproof pan. Drizzle with oil and sprinkle with red pepper flakes, salt, and pepper. Roast until garlic is soft and golden, 25 minutes.
Meanwhile, cook pasta in a large pot of boiling, salted water, until firm to the bite. Drain. Return pasta with tomatoes and garlic to the warm pasta pot. Toss well to coat. Sprinkle with basil. Serve immediately.

WHICH PASTA?
Strands—spaghettini, spaghetti.

THINK AHEAD
Roast tomatoes and garlic up to 1 day in advance. Cover and refrigerate. Reheat in preheated 400°F oven for 10 minutes.

SLOW COOK
GOLDEN GARLIC AND ONION

SERVES 4

4 tbsp (½ stick) butter
3 tbsp extra virgin olive oil
8 garlic cloves, finely chopped
1lb onions (about 2 medium-sized
  onions), finely sliced
1 tsp sugar
salt
½ cup dry white wine
¾ cup heavy cream
black pepper
¼ cup freshly grated Parmesan, plus
  additional to serve
1lb dried pasta

Melt butter and oil in a heavy-bottomed pot over low heat. Add garlic, onion, sugar, and 1 tsp salt. Cover and cook gently, stirring occasionally, until very soft, 30 minutes. Add 1–2 tbsp hot water to the pan, if necessary, to prevent browning. Uncover and turn the heat to medium high. Add wine and simmer until just evaporated, 2 minutes. Stir the cream into the finished sauce. Heat through and simmer until just thickened, 1–2 minutes. Add salt and pepper to taste. Meanwhile, cook pasta in a large pot of boiling, salted water, until firm to the bite. Drain and add pasta with Parmesan to the hot sauce. Toss well to coat. Serve immediately with additional Parmesan.

WHICH PASTA?
Strands or medium ribbons—spaghetti, paglia e fieno, fettuccine, tagliatelle.

THINK AHEAD
Make sauce up to 4 days in advance, omitting the cream. Cool sauce completely. Cover and refrigerate. Reheat and add cream just before serving. Finish as directed.

COOK'S NOTE
This is one of the traditional sauces from Emilia Romagna. Garlic is used very sparingly in this region. But we find that because the garlic is cooked for a long time in this dish, its flavor mellows and combines well with the onion.

VARIATION
GOLDEN GARLIC, ONION, AND FENNEL
Reduce the quantity of onions to 8oz (about 1 medium-sized onion). Add 1 finely chopped large fennel bulb to the pan with the garlic, onions, sugar, and salt. Cook and finish sauce as directed.

PASTA WITH PEPPERS AND EGGPLANT

PEPPERS AND EGGPLANT IN THE PASTA PANTRY

Choose eggplants with smooth, glossy, and unblemished skins. There is no need to salt and degorge the eggplant before using. The bitter juices that made this process necessary in the past have been bred out of most modern eggplant varieties.

Peppers should be shiny, firm, and crisp, with no wrinkles. Hold a pepper in your hand before buying. The heavier the pepper, the better it is, as it will have meatier and juicier flesh. Color is an indication of ripeness, so, for optimum sweetness, choose the deepest red peppers.

Roasting and peeling peppers is well worth the extra effort. Roasting peppers brings out their flavor, while peeling removes the papery, indigestible skin.

Roast peppers whole under a preheated broiler, turning as needed, until charred all over, 10–15 minutes. Wrap in a plastic bag or place in a bowl with a plate on top and leave until cool. The steam released by the peppers as they cool will loosen the skin.

To peel, remove pepper from bag or bowl. Peel off the charred skin, using the tip of a small knife. Scrape rather than rinse off any remaining bits of skin; rinsing washes away flavor. You can roast and peel peppers up to a week in advance. Cover with oil and refrigerate.

Although roasted peppers in jars are a quick substitute for fresh roast peppers, they never really lose their distinctive "jar" taste.

QUICK COOK
ROASTED PEPPER

SERVES 4

4 red peppers
6 tbsp extra virgin olive oil
2 garlic cloves, finely chopped
½ tsp crushed red pepper flakes
salt, black pepper
1lb dried pasta
3 tbsp chopped fresh flat-leaf parsley
additional olive oil, optional

Roast, peel, and seed peppers (see page 157). Cut into strips 2 inches long and ½ inch wide. Heat oil in a skillet. Add garlic and red pepper flakes and cook over medium high heat until fragrant, 1 minute. Add peppers and cook, stirring occasionally, until flavors are blended, 4 minutes. Add salt and pepper to taste. Meanwhile, cook pasta in a large pot of boiling, salted water, until firm to the bite. Drain. Add drained pasta with parsley to the hot peppers. Toss well. Drizzle with 2 tbsp additional olive oil, if using. Serve immediately.

WHICH PASTA?
Large tubes—penne, rigatoni.

EGGPLANT WITH CHILI AND GARLIC

SERVES 4

½ cup extra virgin olive oil
5 cups eggplant, cut into ½-inch dice
4 garlic cloves, crushed
½ tsp crushed red pepper flakes
2 tbsp tomato paste
1 tsp dried oregano
salt, black pepper
1lb dried pasta
additional extra virgin olive oil for pasta

Heat oil in a skillet. Add eggplant, garlic, and red pepper flakes and cook, stirring frequently over high heat, until golden, 5–7 minutes. Turn down heat to medium low. Stir in tomato paste and oregano and cook, stirring occasionally, until eggplant dice are soft and cooked through, 10 minutes. Add 2 tbsp hot water to the pan if the eggplant begins to stick. Add salt and pepper to taste. Meanwhile, cook pasta in a large pot of boiling, salted water, until firm to the bite. Drain. Add pasta with 2 tbsp additional olive oil to the hot sauce. Toss well to coat. Serve immediately.

WHICH PASTA?
Tubes or shapes—penne, rigatoni, orecchiette, conchiglie, fusilli.

COOKS' NOTE
To enhance the flavor of the spicy red pepper flakes with the eggplant, we like to use a slightly peppery Tuscan or Pugliese olive oil.

VARIATIONS
SICILIAN EGGPLANT WITH GARLIC
Add 2 tbsp capers and 10 sliced pitted black olives, such as kalamata or gaeta, with the tomato paste and oregano. Finish as directed.

EGGPLANT WITH MOLTEN MOZZARELLA
Make sauce as directed. Stir 2 cups diced mozzarella into the finished sauce and heat gently until just melting, 1 minute. Add drained pasta to the hot sauce, omitting the additional olive oil. Finish as directed.

SPICY EGGPLANT WITH GARLIC, BASIL, AND PINE NUTS
Make sauce as directed. Add the drained pasta with 2 tbsp pine nuts and 1 handful torn fresh basil to the hot sauce.

EGGPLANT WITH GARLIC AND RICOTTA
Make sauce as directed. Stir ½ cup ricotta into the finished sauce and heat gently until warm through, 1 minute. Add drained pasta with 3 tbsp freshly grated Pecorino to the hot sauce, omitting the additional olive oil.

ROASTED VEGETABLES WITH GREEN OLIVES AND RICOTTA

SERVES 4

1 eggplant, cut into ½-inch cubes
1 red or yellow pepper, seeded
   and cut into ½-inch pieces
1 small fennel bulb, cut into
   ½-inch pieces
4 small ripe tomatoes, cut
   into quarters
6 whole garlic cloves, peeled
½ tsp crushed red pepper flakes
5 tbsp extra virgin olive oil
salt, black pepper
1lb dried pasta
additional extra virgin olive oil for
   tossing
1 cup pitted green olives
½ cup ricotta
1 handful fresh basil leaves
freshly grated Parmesan to serve

Preheat oven to 400°F.
Toss eggplant, red pepper, fennel,
tomatoes, and garlic with red pepper
flakes and oil to coat well. Spread out on
a baking sheet. Sprinkle with salt and
pepper. Roast until soft and lightly
charred, 20–25 minutes. Meanwhile,
cook pasta in a large pot of boiling, salted
water, until firm to the bite. Drain.
Return drained pasta to the warm pasta
pot and toss in 2 tbsp additional olive oil.
Add roasted vegetables to pasta and toss
well to coat. Add olives, ricotta, and
basil. Serve immediately with Parmesan.

WHICH PASTA?
Medium tubes—macaroni, pennette, cavatelli.

THINK AHEAD
Roast vegetables up to 1 day in advance. Cover
and refrigerate. Reheat in 400°F oven for
10 minutes before tossing with cooked pasta.

RED PEPPER PESTO

SERVES 4

2 large red peppers
2 garlic cloves
5 tbsp pine nuts, preferably toasted
   (see page 161)
¼ tsp crushed red pepper flakes
½ tsp balsamic vinegar
5 tbsp extra virgin olive oil
salt, black pepper
1lb dried pasta
freshly grated Parmesan to serve

Roast, peel, and seed peppers (see page 157). Place peppers, garlic, pine nuts, red
pepper flakes, vinegar, and oil in a food processor; pulse until smooth. Add salt and
pepper to taste. Meanwhile, cook pasta in a large pot of boiling, salted water, until
firm to the bite. Drain, reserving ½ cup pasta water. Return drained pasta to the
warm pasta pot and add red pepper pesto. Toss well to coat adding reserved water as
needed. Serve immediately with Parmesan.

WHICH PASTA?
Strands or tubes—spaghetti, spaghettini, penne.

THINK AHEAD
Make pesto up to 3 days in advance. Cover and refrigerate.

SLOW COOK
ROASTED PEPPER AND TOMATO

SERVES 4

2 red peppers
6 tbsp extra virgin olive oil
1 garlic clove, crushed
¼ tsp crushed red pepper flakes
6 medium tomatoes, peeled,
  seeded, and chopped
salt, black pepper
1lb dried pasta

Roast, peel, and seed peppers (see page 157) and finely chop. Heat oil in a skillet. Add garlic and red pepper flakes and cook over medium heat until fragrant, 1 minute. Add tomatoes and cook, stirring occasionally, until thick, 20 minutes. Add peppers and cook to heat through and blend flavors, 5–10 minutes. Add salt and pepper to taste. Meanwhile, cook pasta in a large pot of boiling, salted water, until firm to the bite. Drain. Add drained pasta to the hot sauce. Toss well to coat. Serve immediately.

WHICH PASTA?
Strands or tubes—spaghetti, penne, cavatelli.

THINK AHEAD
Make sauce up to 3 days in advance. Cover and refrigerate.

COOKS' NOTE
A peppery Tuscan olive oil will enhance—and stand up to—the flavor of this lively, gutsy pasta sauce.

SLOW COOK
ROASTED VEGETABLES AL FORNO

SERVES 4

1 medium eggplant, cut into
  ½-inch dice
2 red peppers, seeded and cut into
  ½-inch dice
2 garlic cloves, crushed
¼ tsp crushed red pepper flakes
3 tbsp extra virgin olive oil
salt, black pepper
1lb dried pasta
1 recipe simmered tomato sauce
  (see page 42)
½ cup ricotta
4oz mozzarella, sliced
6 tbsp freshly grated Parmesan

Preheat oven to 400°F.
Toss eggplant and pepper pieces with garlic, red pepper flakes, and oil to coat well. Spread out evenly on a baking sheet. Sprinkle with salt and pepper. Roast until soft and lightly charred, 20–25 minutes. Meanwhile, cook pasta in a large pot of boiling, salted water, until just firm to the bite. Drain pasta and combine with with tomato sauce and roasted vegetables. Toss well to coat. Add salt and pepper to taste. Place half the tossed pasta in an oiled 8 x 8 x 2-inch ovenproof dish. Cover with ricotta, mozzarella, and half the Parmesan. Top with remaining pasta. Sprinkle with remaining Parmesan. Bake until golden and bubbling, 10 minutes. Let stand for 5 minutes before serving.

WHICH PASTA?
Large tubes or shells—rigatoni, penne, conchiglie.

THINK AHEAD
Assemble, cover unbaked and refrigerate up to 8 hours in advance. Alternatively, cover unbaked and freeze up to 3 weeks in advance. Defrost overnight in refrigerator. Cook in preheated 400°F oven for 30 minutes.

FRESH & FILLED PASTA

FRESH EGG PASTA

SERVES 4

2½ cups Italian 00 (doppio zero) or all-purpose flour
½ tsp salt
3 eggs
additional flour for dusting

ESSENTIAL EQUIPMENT
pasta machine

Mix the flour and salt into a bowl. Make a well in the center of the flour. Add eggs to the well. With a fork, beat the eggs and gradually draw in the flour. With your hands, mix in as much of the flour as needed to make a rough dough. You may not need to incorporate all of the flour. Or if the dough is too sticky, you may need to sprinkle over a little extra flour.

As soon as the dough begins to form a ball, turn it out onto a work surface lightly dusted with flour.

Knead the dough by pushing it away from you with the heel of your hand. Knead until smooth, elastic, and no longer sticky, 10 minutes. Wrap in plastic wrap and let rest for at least 30 minutes or up to 4 hours.

COOKS' NOTE

The finest fresh pasta is always made at home. Homemade fresh pasta is simple, fun, and very satisfying to make. We advise making fresh pasta by hand rather than in a food processor.

Eggs vary in size and different flours will absorb different quantities of liquid on different days, depending on whether you are working in a dry or humid atmosphere. It's always easier to add more flour to a dough that is too soft than correct a dough that is too stiff. Working by hand allows you to adjust the quantity of flour as you go along.

ROLLING OUT FRESH PASTA

Set the pasta machine rollers on their widest setting. Cut the dough into 4 equal-sized pieces. Lightly dust 1 piece of dough with flour and flatten with your hand. Keep the remaining pieces wrapped in plastic wrap. Feed 1 piece pasta dough through the rollers. Place the rolled strip flat on the table and fold in half. Feed the folded dough through the rollers again. Give the dough a quarter turn before feeding it each time through the machine, to ensure that it is evenly kneaded. Repeat folding and rolling out 5 or 6 times until the dough is smooth and silky. Reset the rollers to the next setting and feed the dough through the settings until you achieve the desired thickness (see below for tagliatelle, tagliolini, or lasagne; see page 146 for ravioli). If the dough sticks to the machine, dust both sides lightly with flour.

THINK AHEAD

Make, roll, and cut dough up to 5 days in advance. Let dry out, then store at room temperature in single layers on paper towels set over a tray. Cover with a clean dish towel. Alternatively, freeze for up to 4 months. Let dry out, then place in freezer bags or an airtight container. Freeze.

FRESH TAGLIATELLE OR TAGLIOLINI

Roll the dough through the machine on the second to thinnest setting. Lay each pasta sheet on a clean dish towel, letting about one third of its length hang down over the edge of the work surface. Leave until the pasta is dry to the touch but still pliable, about 10–30 minutes. Feed each sheet of dough through the broad cutters of the machine for tagliatelle or through the narrow ones for tagliolini.

As the strips emerge, catch them on your hand. Sprinkle with a little semolina or all-purpose flour, then coil loosely into a bundle. Place on a clean dish towel and repeat with remaining dough. The pasta strands are now ready to be cooked. Alternatively, place in a single layer on clean dish towels until dry, about 24 hours.

FRESH LASAGNE

Roll out the dough on the last setting of the machine. Cut each pasta sheet into squares measuring about 5 x 3½ inches. Cook immediately or let dry as for tagliatelle or tagliolini.

FRESH RAVIOLI

SERVES 4

1 recipe pasta dough (see page 144)
1 recipe pasta filling (see page 147)
all-purpose flour or semolina for dusting

ESSENTIAL EQUIPMENT
pasta machine, pastry brush, fluted pastry wheel

Roll the dough through the machine on the second to thinnest setting (see page 145). Cut the dough sheets into 20-inch lengths. Cover the dough sheets with plastic wrap to keep them pliable until you are ready to shape them.

Fold the sheet in half to make a crease down the center. Unfold. Using the crease as a guide, place teaspoonfuls of the filling at 1½-inch intervals in 2 rows along opposite sides of the crease. Lightly brush the pasta around the filling with water. Lay over a second pasta sheet to cover the filling. With your fingertips, press gently around each mound of filling to seal the dough and to push out any pockets of air. Cut into squares with a fluted pastry wheel.

Place the squares upside down on a clean dish towel, making sure they do not touch. Repeat with remaining dough. The ravioli are now ready to be cooked. Alternatively, let dry on clean dish towels, turning over occasionally, until the dough has dried out completely, about 24 hours.

Cook the ravioli in gently boiling, salted water under tender to the bite, 4–7 minutes. To drain, scoop out with a slotted spoon and shake off excess water. Place in a warmed bowl and toss gently to coat with sauce. Serve immediately.

THINK AHEAD
Make ravioli up to 3 days in advance. Let dry out, then store on layers of waxed paper in an airtight container in the refrigerator. Alternatively, freeze for up to 2 months. Spread ravioli in a single layer on a baking sheet, making sure that the edges are not touching. Place in freezer uncovered until hard, 30 minutes. Once the ravioli are frozen, pack into zip-lock bags or an airtight container and return to the freezer. Frozen ravioli should be cooked from frozen, allowing an extra 5 minutes of cooking time.

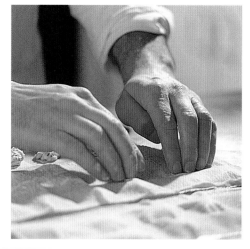

GREENS, PARMESAN, AND RICOTTA FILLING

SERVES 4

2lbs spinach or swiss chard, washed and stemmed
1 cup ricotta
8 tbsp freshly grated Parmesan
salt, pepper, nutmeg
2 eggs

Wash but do not dry spinach. Place wet spinach in a covered pan over a medium heat. Cook, stirring occasionally, until tender, 5 minutes. Drain and leave to cool. Squeeze out excess water with your hands. Chop finely and combine with ricotta and Parmesan. Add salt, pepper, and nutmeg to taste. Add eggs and mix to a stiff paste.

WHICH SAUCE?
Sizzling Sage Butter (see page 108), Butter and Parmesan (see page 47), Fresh Tomato (see page 37).

VARIATIONS

RICOTTA AND HERB FILLING

Replace spinach with 2 handfuls chopped fresh basil or parsley. Combine basil or parsley with ricotta and Parmesan. Finish as directed.

PORCINI MUSHROOM FILLING

SERVES 4

1 cup dried porcini mushrooms
3 tbsp olive oil
2 garlic cloves, finely chopped
1 shallot, finely chopped
1½ lbs cremini or portobello mushrooms, finely chopped
2 tbsp finely chopped fresh flat-leaf parsley

Soak porcini (see page 156) and finely chop them. Heat oil in a skillet. Add garlic and shallots and cook over medium high heat until fragrant, 1 minute. Add mushrooms and porcini and cook, stirring frequently, until crisp, 10 minutes. Add parsley and salt and pepper to taste. Leave to cool completely before using to fill ravioli.

WHICH SAUCE?
Fresh Tomato (see page 37), Butter and Parmesan (see page 47), All'Alfredo (see page 53).

THINK AHEAD
Make fillings up to 1 day in advance. Cover and refrigerate.

THINK AHEAD TIPS

COOKING PASTA FOR A BAKED DISH

When cooking pasta for a dish that will require further cooking, such as in a baked or layered pasta dish, the cooking time should be cut by approximately a third. Depending on the kind of pasta you are cooking, this means you should begin checking for doneness (see page 23) a couple of minutes early. Remove and drain the pasta when it is still slightly hard at the center.

PREPARING AN UNBAKED PASTA DISH FOR THE FREEZER

When preparing baked pasta dishes, such as lasagne, ahead of time, you will get better results if you prepare the recipe and freeze it before baking.

Line the casserole dish with heavy-duty aluminum foil, allowing enough foil to come over the sides of the dish to cover and seal the food.

Assemble the recipe. Be sure that all the ingredients are at room temperature before placing it in the freezer. Fold the additional foil over the top and cover tightly with plastic wrap to ensure that it is airtight. Place in the freezer.

If you wish to use the casserole dish while the assembled recipe is stored in the freezer, line the baking dish as instructed above, but do not cover the top with the extended foil at the sides. Instead, freeze until solid, then use the sides to lift the frozen recipe out of the casserole dish. Cover the frozen recipe with the foil sides to seal. Place in a large zip-lock freezer bag and return to the freezer until ready to use.

DEFROSTING AN UNBAKED PASTA DISH

Remove from freezer bag and place the frozen dish in the casserole in which it will be baked. Place in the refrigerator and allow the dish to thaw overnight, before baking.

Allow frozen pasta sauces to thaw overnight in the refrigerator.

When reheating a sauce, especially when it has been frozen, additional liquid may be needed to return the sauce to the proper consistency.

In the case of rich cream-based or meat sauces, use a few tablespoons of warm milk to add moisture and to retain the rich flavor. In the case of olive oil and tomato based sauces, remember to reserve about half a cup of the pasta water before draining the pasta. Use this, or part of it, to add both moisture and flavor back to the reheated sauce.

MAKING AND FREEZING PASTA SAUCES

Be sure that the sauce has cooled completely before storing it in the freezer.

Choose a container for freezing that has a capacity as close to the actual volume of the sauce prepared as possible. The more oxygen permitted to surround frozen food, the greater the chance of freezer burn and spoilage.

The best way to freeze anything is in a zip-lock freezer bag. Transfer the cooled sauce to a zip-lock freezer bag, expelling as much air as possible before sealing it. Place on a plate in the freezer until frozen solid then remove the plate.

PASTA IN THE PANTRY

Fast food doesn't have to mean take-out when you have pasta in the pantry. Perfect for impromptu entertaining, pasta is the original convenience food. A well-stocked pantry is the key. With a few well-chosen staples (see below) in the kitchen cupboard, refrigerator, or freezer, a simple meal can be on the table in the time it takes to boil water.

To save you from scanning the index, we've compiled an easy reference **PASTA PLANNER** (see pages 152–153) that cross-references ingredients with cooking time. You can select recipes at a glance, simply by matching your schedule to the contents of your shopping cart or pantry.

Pasta is unquestionably the most versatile of foods. It is an everyday food and a food for celebrations. It makes a last-minute dinner for one and a satisfying meal for all the family. Refer to **PASTA ON THE MENU** (see pages 154–155) and you'll see that, whatever the season, the occasion, the time available, or the cook's mood, pasta will deliver.

IN THE REFRIGERATOR

PARMESAN
Buy in a piece and store in the warmest section of the refrigerator.

BUTTER
Must be unsalted for pasta sauces.

EGGS
Buy large and choose organic when possible.

CREAM
For cooking, choose heavy cream or crème fraîche. Crème fraîche is a great pantry basic since it keeps longer than regular cream. Sour cream or plain yogurt can be substituted for crème fraîche

LEMONS
Buy unwaxed lemons when possible, but especially when the recipe calls for grated lemon zest. Even better is to buy organic lemons which are not waxed or sprayed with chemicals.

IN THE FREEZER

UNSMOKED PANCETTA
Cut and wrap pancetta in 2-oz pieces. Bacon is an acceptable alternative.

FROZEN PEAS
Choose tiny, young *petits pois* when possible.

PARSLEY
Buy a bunch of flat-leaf Italian parsley, chop and keep in an airtight container for using as needed.

In the Cupboard

Dried Pasta
Have a selection of shapes and a variety of sizes on hand.

Anchovies
Buy in cans or jars. Alternatively, have a tube of anchovy paste in the refrigerator (see page 160).

Tuna
Choose cans of tuna packed in olive oil for best texture and taste. We prefer chunk tuna.

Tomatoes
Choose cans of Italian brands for tastier, juicier tomatoes.

Capers
Buy in jars, in brine or salt (see page 160).

Olives
Good quality pitted black olives in jars or cans, such as kalamata or gaeta, are useful to have on stock in the pasta pantry.

Crushed Red Pepper Flakes
Renew your supply yearly since dried red pepper flakes lose their kick over time.

Dried Porcini
Buy packages with large pieces, which are from the mushroom caps. The smaller, crumblier pieces come from the stalks and have less flavor.

Onions
Small yellow onions are the most useful.

White Wine
Choose a dry, light white wine.

Garlic
Choose milder pink-skinned garlic when possible.

Olive Oil
Always buy extra virgin. We like to have a regular brand on hand for cooking, plus a bottle of premium oil for seasoning cooked foods and drizzling.

Coarse Salt
Kosher salt is the choice of serious cooks because of its fuller flavor.

Black Peppercorns
Always buy whole peppercorns and freshly grind to order.

PASTA PLANNER

	MAKE AHEAD	NO COOK	QUICK COOK	SLOW COOK	AL FORNO
ASPARAGUS			• Asparagus with Cream • Asparagus, Prosciutto & Fresh Herbs		
BASIL	• Simple Basil Pesto	• Simple Basil Pesto • Even Simpler Basil Pesto • Lemon, Basil, & Mascarpone	• Classic Genoese Pesto		
BEEF	• Classic Ragù Bolognese • Lasagne al Forno		• Pizzaiola	• Classic Ragù Bolognese	• Lasagne al Forno
BROCCOLI			• Spicy Broccoli		
BUTTER		• Butter & Parmesan			
CHICKEN	• Chicken, Tomato, & Rosemary Ragù		• Pan-Roasted Chicken with Lemon & Mushrooms	• Chicken, Tomato, & Rosemary Ragù	
CREAM		• Cream & Parmesan	• Golden Saffron • All'Alfredo		
EGGPLANT			• Eggplant with Chili & Garlic	• Roasted Vegetables with Green Olives & Ricotta	• Roasted Vegetables al Forno
GARLIC			• Olio Aglio • Roasted Garlic & Cherry Tomatoes	• Golden Garlic & Onion	
GORGONZOLA	• Four Cheese	• Gorgonzola & Ricotta	• Gorgonzola Cream		• Four Cheese
MOZZARELLA	• Four Cheese • Tomato and Mozzarella al Forno	• Three Cheese • Fresh Tomato with Mozzarella	• Fresh Tomato Sauce with Molten Mozzarella • Pan-Cooked Tomato & Mozzarella	• Tomato & Mozzarella al Forno	• Tomato and Mozzarella al Forno
MUSHROOMS	• Mushroom al Forno		• Wild Mushroom Persillade • Mushroom, White Wine, & Cream		• Mushroom al Forno
DRIED PORCINI	• Tomato with Porcini		• Porcini, White Wine, & Cream		• Mushroom al Forno
PANCETTA			• Carbonara • Crispy Pancetta with Scallions • Amatriciana		
OLIVES	• Chili Olive Pesto • Olive, Anchovy, & Caper Pesto	• Chili Olive Pesto • Olive, Anchovy, & Caper Pesto	• Spicy Lemon Olive • Puttanesca		

	MAKE AHEAD	NO COOK	QUICK COOK	SLOW COOK	AL FORNO
PARSLEY	• Parsley Pesto	• Parsley Pesto • Butter, Parmesan, & Parsley	• Fresh Fragrant Herbs		
PEAS	• Primavera		• Peas, Prosciutto, & Fresh Herbs • Primavera • Butter, Parmesan, & Peas		
PEPPERS	• Roasted Vegetables al Forno • Red Pepper Pesto • Roasted Pepper & Tomato Sauce		• Roasted Vegetables with Green Olives & Ricotta • Red Pepper Pesto	• Roasted Pepper & Tomato Sauce	• Roasted Vegetables al Forno
PROSCIUTTO			• Prosciutto & Cream • Peas, Prosciutto, & Fresh Herbs		
SAUSAGE	• Spicy Sausage Ragù		• Sausage with Cream & Basil	• Spicy Sausage Ragù	
SHRIMP	• Shrimp with Lemon & Basil	• Shrimp with Lemon & Basil	• Spicy Garlic Shrimp with Cherry Tomatoes • Chili Shrimp		
SPINACH	• Spinach & Walnut Pesto • Spinach & Ricotta Lasagne	• Spinach & Walnut Pesto	• Wilted Spinach with Golden Garlic	• Spinach & Ricotta Lasagne	• Spinach & Ricotta Lasagne
SMOKED SALMON		• Smoked Salmon, Vodka, & Dill	• Smoked Salmon with White Wine, Cream, & Chives		
TOMATOES Fresh	• Puttanesca • Arrabbiata • Napolitana • Roasted Tomato		• Fresh Tomato • Puttanesca • Arrabbiata • Napolitana	• Roasted Tomato	
Sun-dried	• Red Pesto • Sun-dried Tomato with Chili, Garlic, and Black Olives	• Red Pesto			
Canned	• Puttanesca • Arrabbiata • Napolitana • Tomato & Mozzarella al Forno • Simmered Tomato		• Puttanesca • Arrabbiata • Napolitana • Pan-Cooked Tomato & Mozzarella	• Tomato & Mozzarella al Forno • Simmered Tomato	• Tomato & Mozzarella al Forno
TUNA	• Tuna with Lemon & Capers • Tuna & Tomato	• Tuna with Lemon & Capers	• Tuna & Tomato		

PASTA ON THE MENU

SHORT ORDER PASTA

In a rush? Try these fast and simple sauces, based on a few fresh ingredients, that are on the table in less than 20 minutes.

Butter, Parmesan, & Asparagus
(See page 47)
Scallops with Garlic &
Crisp Crumbs
(See page 68)
Chicken with Lemon &
Mushrooms
(See page 87)
Lemon, Basil, & Mascarpone
(See page 51)
Fresh Tomato Sauce with
Molten Mozzarella
(See page 37)
Smoked Salmon,
Vodka, & Dill
(See page 64)
Pizzaiola
(See page 83)

PASTA TO CELEBRATE SPRING

Winter is finally over and the season's first fresh roots and shoots appear on the market. Why not celebrate, Italian-style?

Peas, Prosciutto, & Fresh Herbs
(See page 111)
Primavera
(See page 116)
Fava Beans with Pecorino
(See page 123)
Parsley Pesto
(See page 107)
Asparagus with Cream
(See page 112)

PASTA SOLO

There's no need to go without because it's just you at home this evening. Treat yourself! Pasta makes cooking for one fun.

Olio Aglio
(See page 129)
Even Simpler Basil Pesto
(See page 105)
Three Cheese
(See page 49)
Salmon Caviar with
Butter & Chives
(See page 66)
Butter & Parmesan
(See page 47)
Fresh Herbs &
Golden Crumbs
(See page 108)

SELF-SERVE PASTA FOR A BUFFET OUTDOORS

Light, fresh, and mayo-free, these pasta salads are perfect for Italian al fresco dining. Try one or two at your next backyard party.

Fresh Tomato, Arugula, &
Balsamic Vinegar
(See page 33)
Tuna with Lemon & Capers
(See page 64)
Classic Genoese Pesto
(See page 124)
Sun-Dried Tomato with Chili,
Garlic, & Black Olives
(See page 33)

PASTA FOR CHILDREN

Even babies in highchairs love pasta. Try these dishes out on young mouths: they'll soon be firm favorites with all the family.

Simmered Tomato
(See page 42)
Butter, Parmesan, & Peas
(See page 47)
Four Cheese al Forno
(See page 52)
Tuna and Tomato
(See page 69)
Classic Ragù Bolognese
(See page 91)
Napolitana
(See page 35)

DO-AHEAD DINNER PARTY PASTA

Many pasta sauces can be prepared well in advance. Any of these simple recipes will make an elegant opener for six or a nonmeat main for four. Refer to our Think Ahead notes.

Spinach & Walnut Pesto
(See page 107)
Simmered Tomato
with Vodka
(See page 42)
Primavera with Cream
(See page 116)
Roasted Vegetables with
Green Olives & Ricotta
(See page 138)
Roasted Tomato with Pesto
(See page 40)

COLD WEATHER COMFORT PASTA

When the sky's gray and the wind bites, nothing beats a steaming bowl of pasta for lighting up faces around the table.

Spicy Sausage Ragù
(See page 91)
Golden Garlic & Onion
(See page 131)
Braised Umbrian Lentils
(See page 124)
Ragù Al Forno
(See page 92)
Pan-Cooked Tomato & Mozzarella
(See page 39)

IMPROMPTU PASTA

With our well-chosen staples on hand (refer to Pasta in the Pantry on page 150) even the busiest of cooks can create a quick-fix meal in a matter of minutes.

Tuna & Tomato
(See page 69)
All'Alfredo
(See page 53)
Olio Aglio Peperoncino
(See page 129)
Tomatoes with Porcini
(See page 60)
Butter, Parmesan, & Peas
(See page 47)
Spicy Lemon Olive
(See page 101)

PASTA ITALIA

Simple, honest, traditional dishes full of the charm and flavor of Italy.

Napolitana
(See page 35)
Carbonara
(See page 88)
Arrabbiata
(See page 35)
Puttanesca
(See page 34)
Olio Aglio Peperoncino
(See page 129)
Amatriciana
(See page 87)

PASTA TO IMPRESS

Here is a repertoire of simple but stylish pasta dishes that make you look good, whether you're out to impress friends, family, your boss, or your date!

Spicy Garlic Shrimp with Cherry Tomatoes
(See page 73)
Pan-Roasted Chicken with Garlic & Shallots
(See page 84)
Seafood Extravaganza
(See page 77)
Scallops with Crème Fraîche & Dill
(See page 72)
Smoked Salmon with White Wine, Cream, & Chives
(See page 70)
Wild Mushroom Persillade
(See page 57)

PASTA FOR CROWDS

Easy and economical, pasta can feed hoards of hungry mouths, without breaking the bank or causing sleepless nights. Refer to our Think Ahead notes.

Spinach & Ricotta Lasagne
(See page 118)
Mushroom al Forno
(See page 60)
Tomato & Mozzarella al Forno
(See page 39)
Roasted Vegetables al Forno
(See page 141)
Classic Lasagne al Forno
(See page 95)

SUMMER WEEKEND PASTA

Light dishes with bright tastes for lazy lunches in the sunshine.

Fresh Tomato Sauce with Pesto
(See page 37)
Eggplant with Garlic, Basil, & Pine Nuts
(See page 137)
Chili Shrimp
(See page 70)
Fresh Tomato, Red Onion, & Basil
(See page 33)
Red Pesto with Arugula
(See page 31)
Spicy Garlic Scallops
(See page 73)

THE SKILLS - TOP TIPS

PEELING TOMATOES

Cut a small cross on the base of each tomato. Drop tomatoes into boiling water. Remove when you see the edges of the cross begin to loosen, 10–20 seconds, depending on the ripeness. Drain, then immerse tomatoes in cold water. Peel off the loosened skins, using the tip of a knife.

SOAKING DRIED MUSHROOMS

Place mushrooms in a small bowl and add boiling water to cover. Leave for 30 minutes. Strain soaking liquid through a cheesecloth-lined strainer before using.

SEEDING TOMATOES

Cut the tomato in half crosswise. Gently squeeze each tomato half, pushing out the seeds with your fingertips.

PEELING A GARLIC CLOVE

Set the flat side of the knife on top and strike it with your fist. This action will loosen the skin, allowing it to peel away easily. Discard the skin.

CHOPPING AN ONION

Peel the onion, leaving the root end on. Cut the onion in half and lay one half, cut side down, on a chopping board. With a sharp knife, cut horizontally toward the root end, and then vertically. Be sure to cut just to the root but not through it. Finally, cut the onion crosswise into diced pieces.

PEELING PEPPERS

Broil peppers under a preheated broiler. Turn as needed until blackened on all sides, 10–15 minutes. Place in a plastic bag or a bowl with a plate on top and allow to cool. Peel off the skin using the tip of a small knife. Cut the peppers into quarters and remove the core. Scrape away seeds and discard.

THE CHOP - SIZE GUIDE

All pictures shown are life size

ROUGHLY CHOPPED PARSLEY

FINELY CHOPPED PARSLEY

DICED TOMATO

DICED CARROT AND CELERY

SLICED ONION

CHOPPED ONION

FINELY CHOPPED ONION

FINELY CHOPPED GARLIC

NOTES FROM THE COOKS ON INGREDIENTS

ANCHOVY FILLETS can be soaked in milk for 10 minutes before using if you find the flavor too pungent. Use ½ tsp of anchovy paste as an alternative to 1 anchovy fillet when called for as an ingredient in a cooked pasta sauce.

BUTTER should always be unsalted when working with the recipes in this book.

CAPERS must be drained before using when they come packed in brine. We prefer to use capers preserved in salt, which are harder to find but worth the effort, since they retain more of their natural flavor than those packed in brine. Capers preserved in salt must be rinsed and dried on paper towels before using.

CHEESES that are most suitable for the pasta pantry are discussed in more detail on page 46. **FONTINA** is a semisoft cheese made from cow's milk with an aromatic flavor and great melting properties. Look for authentic Italian Fontina when possible and avoid the more widely available Danish variety. Its name is a derivative of *fondere*—to melt.
Gruyère is a hard Swiss cheese with a sweet, nutty flavor. It melts without becoming oily or rubbery and is a good alternative to Fontina cheese.
Parmesan is a hard Italian cheese with a rich, sharp flavor that is nothing like the stale, acrid taste of grated Parmesan sold in a tub. Always buy Italian Parmesan. Buy in a piece and grate it as required. See page 46 for further information.
Pecorino Romano is a hard Italian cheese with a tangy, piquant flavor that pairs well with the spicy pasta sauces originating from Southern Italy. Use Parmesan as an alternative.
Provolone is made from cow's milk and has a light ivory color, a mild flavor, and smooth texture.
Mascarpone is the creamiest of Italian cheeses. It was originally made as a fresh cheese only in the winter months, and had to be consumed within a couple of days. Now it is manufactured with a UHT process and sold in tubs, allowing it to be a "long-life" product. It does not have the same superior taste of the highly perishable "fresh," but is an adequate substitute.
Ricotta is used extensively in Italian cooking. If you can, buy it fresh from authentic Italian food stores, but be sure to taste it for freshness before buying and to use it with in 48 hours.

CRUSHED RED PEPPER FLAKES are a widely available hot seasoning often used as an ingredient in pasta sauces. Called peperoncino in Italian.

DRIED BREADCRUMBS should be made with good white bread that is 2–3 days old. Cut the bread into pieces and pulse in a food processor or a blender until reduced to fine crumbs. Spread crumbs on a baking sheet and bake in a preheated 300°F oven for a 2–3 minutes, until dry and crisp. Make a large batch and store in an airtight container for up to 1 month.

EGGS are always large eggs. Recipes made with uncooked egg, such as Carbonara (see page 88) and Cream and Parmesan (see page 49) should not be made for children, the elderly, or anyone with a weakened imune system.

FLOUR for making fresh pasta is ideally Italian pasta flour, **Tipo 00/Doppio Zero** (double zero), which can be found at some supermarkets and in Italian specialty stores. Alternatively, use all-purpose flour. **Semolina** flour is a useful addition when making fresh pasta dough. Sprinkle liberally over freshly made pasta to prevent it from sticking. We recommend buying Italian semolina whenever possible.

GARLIC are always medium-sized cloves unless we indicate otherwise.

KOSHER SALT is always preferred in all recipes. Buy it in flakes or crystals. See page 21 for more information.

LEMONS for lemon zest should be unwaxed. When possible buy organic lemons since they are both unwaxed and unsprayed.

MUSHROOMS should never be rinsed in water. To clean mushrooms properly, simply wipe gently with a damp dish towel. See page 56 for more information on the varieties of mushrooms best suited for pasta.

NUTMEG is sold ground or whole. We recommend buying whole nutmeg and grating it freshly as needed. The flavor of freshly grated nutmeg is vastly superior to anything ground.

OLIVES—see information about the olive varieties best suited for pasta on page 98.

PINE NUTS are the most flavorful when they are toasted over medium heat in a dry cast-iron frying pan until golden and fragrant, 5 minutes. Shake the pan frequently. Remove from the pan immediately.

PROSCIUTTO is an Italian air-dried, salt cured ham. See page 80 for more information.

SHRIMP when large should be deveined after removing the shell. Run a small, sharp knife over the top edge of the peeled shrimp and rinse away the grit.

SUN-DRIED TOMATOES are most commonly sold marinated in oil; drain before using. We like to use packaged dried tomatoes that are partly dried and not preserved in olive oil. These must be reconstituted in equal parts vinegar and water for 3 hours. Dry with paper towels and use immediately, or store covered in extra virgin olive oil with 2 or 3 cloves of garlic.

INDEX

A

al dente 23
al forno *see* baked pasta dishes
All'Alfredo 53
Amatriciana 86-7
anchovies 101, 150, 160
  Olive, anchovy, & caper pesto 100
  Puttanesca 34
  Spicy broccoli with golden garlic &
    anchovies 112
  Spicy lemon olive 101
Arrabbiata 35
arugula
  Fresh tomato, arugula, & balsamic
    vinegar 33
  Gorgonzola, ricotta, & arugula 50
  Red pesto with arugula 31
asparagus
  Asparagus with cream 112
  Asparagus, prosciutto, & fresh
    herbs 111
  Butter, Parmesan, & asparagus 47
  Primavera 116-17
  Primavera with cream 116
  Primavera pesto 116

B

bacon 80
  Amatriciana 86-7
  Carbonara 88-9
  Classic ragù bolognese 91
  Crispy pancetta & scallions 83
  Roasted tomato with crispy pancetta 40
baked pasta dishes 148
  Classic Italian-American lasagne 95
  Classic lasagne al forno 94-5
  Eggplant, basil, & mozzarella
    lasagne 118
  Four cheeses al forno 52
  Mushroom al forno 60-1
  Mushroom, garlic, & parsley lasagne 118
  Ragù al forno 92
  Roasted vegetables al forno 141
  Spinach & ricotta lasagne 118-19
  Spinach, Gogonzola, & pine nut
    lasagne 118
  Tomato & mozzarella al forno 38-9
basil 104
  Basil pesto cream 105
  Basil ricotta pesto 105
  Best basil pesto 105
  Classic Genoese pesto 124
  Eggplant, basil, & mozzarella
    lasagne 118
  Even simpler basil pesto 105
  Fresh herb olive oil 99
  Fresh tomato, red onion, & basil 33
  Gorgonzola, ricotta, & basil 50

Lemon, basil, & mascarpone 51
  Primavera pesto 116
  Red pesto with basil 31
  Ricotta & herb filling, for ravioli 147
  Roasted tomato with ricotta & basil 40
  Sausage with cream & basil 84
  Shrimp with lemon & basil 66-7
  Simple basil pesto 105
  Spicy eggplant with garlic, basil, &
    pine nuts 137
  Zucchini & basil with cream 110-11
bay, Simmered tomato with cinnamon
  & bay 42
beans *see* fava beans; green beans
bechamel
  Classic lasagne al forno 94-5
  Eggplant, basil, & mozzarella
    lasagne 118
  Mushroom al forno 60-1
  Mushroom, garlic, & parsley lasagne 118
  Ragù al forno 92
  Spinach & ricotta lasagne 118-19
  Spinach, Gogonzola, & pine nut
    lasagne 118
beef *see* steak
Best basil pesto 105
bite, of cooked pasta 23
boiling pasta 22
Braised Umbrian lentils 124-5
breadcrumbs 160
  Fresh herbs & golden crumbs 108
  Scallops with garlic & crisp crumbs 68
broccoli 104
  Spicy broccoli with golden
    garlic 112-13
  Spicy broccoli with golden garlic &
    anchovies 112
  Spicy broccoli rabe with golden
    garlic 112
butter 150, 160
  All'Alfredo 53
  Best basil pesto 105
  Butter & Parmesan 47
  Butter, Parmesan, & asparagus 47
  Butter, Parmesan, & ham 47
  Butter, Parmesan, & parsley 47
  Butter, Parmesan, & peas 47
  Four cheeses al forno 52
  Golden saffron 52
  Gorgonzola & ricotta 50
  Gorgonzola cream 51
  Gorgonzola, ricotta, & baby spinach 50
  Gorgonzola, ricotta, & basil 50
  Gorgonzola, ricotta, & arugula 50
  Salmon caviar with butter & chives 66
  Sizzling sage butter 108-9
  Three cheese 49
buying pasta 14

C

capers 150, 160
  Olive, anchovy, & caper pesto 100
  Piquant fresh tomato 37
  Piquant tuna with tomatoes 69
  Pizzaiola 82-3
  Puttanesca 34
  Sicilian eggplant with garlic 137
  Tuna with lemon & capers 64
Carbonara 88-9
castelluccio lentils 122
  Braised Umbrian lentils 124-5
cauliflower 104
  Spicy cauliflower with golden
    garlic 112
chard, Greens, Parmesan, & ricotta
  filling, for ravioli 147
cheese 46, 160
  All'Alfredo 53
  Basil ricotta pesto 105
  Butter & Parmesan 47
  Butter, Parmesan, & asparagus 47
  Butter, Parmesan, & ham 47
  Butter, Parmesan, & parsley 47
  Butter, Parmesan, & peas 47
  Classic Italian-American lasagne 95
  Cream & Parmesan 48-9
  Eggplant, basil, & mozzarella
    lasagne 118
  Eggplant with garlic & ricotta 137
  Eggplant with molten
    mozzarella 137
  Fava beans with Pecorino 123
  Four cheeses al forno 52
  Fresh tomato & mozzarella 33
  Fresh tomato with molten
    mozzarella 37
  Fresh tomato with ricotta 37
  Gorgonzola & ricotta 50
  Gorgonzola cream 51
  Gorgonzola, ricotta, & baby spinach 50
  Gorgonzola, ricotta, & basil 50
  Gorgonzola, ricotta, & arugula 50
  Greens, Parmesan, & ricotta filling,
    for ravioli 147
  Lemon, basil, & mascarpone 51
  Mushroom, garlic, & parsley
    lasagne 118
  Pan-cooked tomato &
    mozzarella 38-9
  Ricotta & herb filling, for ravioli 147
  Roasted tomato with ricotta & basil 40
  Roasted vegetables al forno 141
  Roasted vegetables with green olives
    & ricotta 138-9
  Spinach & ricotta lasagne 118-19
  Spinach, Gogonzola, & pine nut
    lasagne 118

Three cheese 49
Tomato & mozzarella al forno 38-9
cherry tomatoes
    Roasted garlic & cherry tomatoes 130
    Shrimp with lemon & basil 66-7
    Spicy garlic shrimp with cherry
        tomatoes 73
    Spicy garlic scallops 73
    Tuna with lemon & capers 64
chicken
    Chicken with lemon & mushrooms 87
    Chicken, tomato, & rosemary ragù 92-3
    Pan-roasted chicken with garlic &
        shallots 84-5
chicken livers, Venetian-style chicken
    liver 88
chickpeas 122
    Chickpeas with rosemary, chili, &
        garlic 123
Chili olive pesto 100
Chili shrimp 70-1
Chili squid 70-1
chives
    Salmon caviar with butter & chives 66
    Smoked salmon with white wine,
        cream, & chives 70
choosing pasta 14-15
chopping & peeling 156-9
cinnamon, Simmered tomato with
    cinnamon & bay 42
clams
    Red clam sauce 74
    Seafood extravaganza 76-7
    White clam sauce 68
Classic genoese pesto 124
Classic Italian-American lasagne 95
Classic lasagne al forno 94-5
Classic ragù bolognese 91
colanders 10
cooking techniques 7
    cooking pasta 8, 21-5, 148
    freezing & defrosting 148-9
    no-cook lasagne 95, 118
    paglia e fieno (straw & hay) 66, 131
    preparing ingredients 156-9
cooking times 7
    pasta planner chart 152-3
crayfish, Seafood
    extravaganza 76-7
cream 150
    All'Alfredo 53
    Asparagus with cream 112
    Cream & Parmesan 48-9
    Golden garlic & onion 131
    Golden saffron 52
    Gorgonzola cream 51
    Mushroom, white wine, & cream 58-9
    Pan-roasted chicken with garlic &
        shallots 84-5
    Porcini, white wine, & cream 58-9
    Primavera with cream 116
    Prosciutto & cream 81
    Sausage with cream & basil 84

Simmered tomato with cream 42
Smoked salmon, vodka, & dill 64-5
Smoked salmon with white wine,
    cream, & chives 70
Zucchini & basil with cream 110-11
crème fraîche
    Basil pesto cream 105
    Scallops with crème fraîche & dill 72
Crispy pancetta & scallions 83

D
defrosting & freezing 148-9
dill
    Scallops with crème fraîche & dill 72
    Smoked salmon, vodka, & dill 64-5
dough preparation, fresh (homemade)
    pasta 144
draining pasta 24
dried pasta 14, 20, 150
durum wheat 14

E
eggs 150, 160
    Carbonara 88-9
    Cream & Parmesan 48-9
    egg pasta, compared to plain pasta 14
    Fresh egg pasta 144-5
    Fresh ravioli 146-7
eggplant 134
    Eggplant, basil, & mozzarella
        lasagne 118
    Eggplant with chili & garlic 136-7
    Eggplant with garlic & ricotta 137
    Eggplant with molten
        mozzarella 137
    Roasted vegetables al forno 141
    Roasted vegetables with green olives
        & ricotta 138-9
    Sicilian eggplant with garlic 137
    Spicy eggplant with garlic, basil, &
        pine nuts 137
equipment 7, 10-13
Even simpler basil pesto 105

F
fava beans 122
    Fava beans with Pecorino 123
fennel
    Golden garlic, onion, & fennel 131
    Roasted vegetables with green olives
        & ricotta 138-9
fillings, for ravioli 147
fish see seafood
flour 160
    Fresh egg pasta 144-5
Fontina 160
    Four cheeses al forno 52
    Three cheese 49
Four cheeses al forno 52
Fragrant fresh herb 107
freezing & defrosting 148-9
Fresh herb olive oil 99
Fresh herbs & golden crumbs 108

fresh pasta
    compared to dried pasta 14
    cooking notes 23
    Fresh egg pasta 144-5
    Fresh ravioli 146-7
    serving quantities 23
Fresh tomato 32-3
Fresh tomato & lemon 33
Fresh tomato & mozzarella 33
Fresh tomato & olives 33
Fresh tomato with molten mozzarella 37
Fresh tomato, red onion, & basil 33
Fresh tomato with ricotta 37
Fresh tomato, arugula, & balsamic
    vinegar 33
Fresh tomato sauce 36-7
Fresh tomato sauce with pesto 37

G
garlic 128, 151, 156, 159, 160
    Chickpeas with rosemary, chili, &
        garlic 123
    Eggplant with chili & garlic 136-7
    Eggplant with garlic & ricotta 137
    Fava beans with Pecorino 123
    Garlic olive oil 99
    Golden garlic & onion 131
    Golden garlic, onion, & fennel 131
    Mushroom, garlic, & parsley
        lasagne 118
    Olio aglio 129
    Olio aglio peperoncino 129
    Olive oil, garlic, & fresh tomato 129
    Olive oil, garlic, & parsley 129
    Pan-roasted chicken with garlic &
        shallots 84-5
    Roasted garlic & cherry tomatoes 130
    Scallops with garlic & crisp
        crumbs 68
    Shredded zucchini with golden
        garlic 114-15
    Sicilian eggplant with garlic 137
    Spicy eggplant with garlic, basil, &
        pine nuts 137
    Spicy broccoli with golden
        garlic 112-13
    Spicy broccoli with golden garlic &
        anchovies 112
    Spicy broccoli rabe with golden
        garlic 112
    Spicy cauliflower with golden
        garlic 112
    Spicy garlic shrimp with cherry
        tomatoes 73
    Spicy garlic scallops 73
    Sun-dried tomato with chili, garlic, &
        black olives 33
    Wilted leeks with golden garlic 115
    Wilted spinach with golden garlic 115
genoese pesto, Classic 124
Golden garlic & onion 131
Golden garlic, onion, & fennel 131
Golden saffron 52

Gorgonzola 46
  Gorgonzola & ricotta 50
  Gorgonzola cream 51
  Gorgonzola, ricotta, & baby
    spinach 50
  Gorgonzola, ricotta, & basil 50
  Gorgonzola, ricotta, & arugula 50
  Spinach, Gogonzola, & pine nut
    lasagne 118
green beans 122
  Classic Genoese pesto 124
  Primavera 116-17
  Primavera with cream 116
  Primavera pesto 116
Greens, Parmesan, & ricotta filling, for
  ravioli 147
Gruyère 160
  Four cheeses al forno 52
  Three cheese 49

H

ham
  Butter, Parmesan, & ham 47
  Zucchini with ham 111
  see also prosciutto
herbs 104
  Asparagus, prosciutto, & fresh
    herbs 111
  Fragrant fresh herb 107
  Fresh herb olive oil 99
  Fresh herbs & golden crumbs 108
  Peas, prosciutto, & fresh herbs 111
  Ricotta & herb filling, for ravioli 147
  see also individual herbs by name
    e.g. basil
homemade pasta 144-7

I

Italian-American lasagne, Classic 95

L

lasagne
  Eggplant, basil, & mozzarella
    lasagne 118
  Classic Italian-American lasagne 95
  Classic lasagne al forno 94-5
  fresh (homemade) 145
  Mushroom, garlic, & parsley
    lasagne 118
  no-cook lasagne, cooks' note 95, 118
  Spinach & ricotta lasagne 118-19
  Spinach, Gogonzola, & pine nut
    lasagne 118
leeks, Wilted leeks with golden
  garlic 115
legumes *see* chickpeas; lentils
lemons 150, 160
  Chicken with lemon & mushrooms 87
  Fresh tomato & lemon 33
  Lemon, basil, & mascarpone 51
  Lemon olive oil 99
  Shrimp with lemon & basil 66-7
  Spicy lemon olive 101

Tuna with lemon & capers 64
lentils 122
  Braised Umbrian lentils 124-5
long pasta 16-17, 24
Luganega sausage 80

M

mascarpone 160
  Lemon, basil, & mascarpone 51
measuring accurately 7
meat 80
  chicken
    Chicken with lemon & mushrooms 87
    Chicken, tomato, & rosemary
      ragù 92-3
    Pan-roasted chicken with garlic &
      shallots 84-5
  chicken livers, Venetian-style chicken
    liver 88
  ham
    Butter, Parmesan, & ham 47
    Zucchini with ham 111
  pancetta or bacon 80, 150
    Amatriciana 86-7
    Carbonara 88-9
    Classic ragù bolognese 91
    Crispy pancetta & scallions 83
    Roasted tomato with crispy
      pancetta 40
  prosciutto 80
    Asparagus, prosciutto, & fresh
      herbs 111
    Peas, prosciutto, & fresh herbs 111
    Prosciutto & cream 81
  sausage 80
    Sausage with cream & basil 84
    Spicy sausage ragù 90-1
  steak
    Classic Italian-American lasagne 95
    Classic lasagne al forno 94-5
    Classic ragù bolognese 91
    Pizzaiola 82-3
    Ragù al forno 92
menu ideas 154-5
mozzarella 46
  Eggplant, basil, & mozzarella
    lasagne 118
  Eggplant with molten
    mozzarella 137
  Classic Italian-American lasagne 95
  Four cheeses al forno 52
  Fresh tomato & mozzarella 33
  Fresh tomato with molten mozzarella 37
  Pan-cooked tomato &
    mozzarella 38-9
  Roasted vegetables al forno 141
  Three cheese 49
  Tomato & mozzarella al forno 38-9
mushrooms 56, 156, 161
  Chicken with lemon & mushrooms 87
  Mushroom al forno 60-1
  Mushroom, garlic, & parsley
    lasagne 118

Mushroom, white wine, & cream 58-9
  Porcini mushroom filling, for
    ravioli 147
  Porcini, white wine, & cream 58-9
  Tomatoes with porcini 60
  Wild mushroom persillade 57
mussels
  Red mussel sauce 74-5
  Seafood extravaganza 76-7
  White clam sauce variation 68

N

Napolitana 35
no-cook lasagne, cooks' note 95, 118

O

olive oil 21, 98, 151
  Fresh herb olive oil 99
  Garlic olive oil 99
  Lemon olive oil 99
  Olio aglio 129
  Olio aglio peperoncino 129
  Olive oil 99
  Olive oil, garlic, & fresh tomato 129
  Olive oil, garlic, & parsley 129
olives 98, 150
  Chili olive pesto 100
  Fresh tomato & olives 33
  Olive, anchovy, & caper pesto 100
  Piquant fresh tomato 37
  Piquant tuna with tomatoes 69
  Pizzaiola 82-3
  Puttanesca 34
  Roasted vegetables with green olives
    & ricotta 138-9
  Sicilian eggplant with garlic 137
  Spicy lemon olive 101
  Sun-dried tomato with chili, garlic, &
    black olives 33
onions 150, 157, 159
  Crispy pancetta & scallions 83
  Fresh tomato, red onion, & basil 33
  Golden garlic & onion 131
  Golden garlic, onion, & fennel 131
  Pan-roasted chicken with garlic &
    shallots 84-5
oven temperatures 7

P

paglia e fieno (straw & hay), cooks'
  note 66, 131
Pan-cooked tomato & mozzarella 38-9
Pan-roasted chicken with garlic &
  shallots 84-5
pancetta 80, 150
  Amatriciana 86-7
  Carbonara 88-9
  Classic ragù bolognese 91
  Crispy pancetta & scallions 83
  Roasted tomato with crispy
    pancetta 40
pans & pan sizes 7, 10-11
pantry staples 150-1

Parmesan 25, 46, 150, 160
  All'Alfredo 53
  Butter & Parmesan 47
  Butter, Parmesan, & asparagus 47
  Butter, Parmesan, & ham 47
  Butter, Parmesan, & parsley 47
  Butter, Parmesan, & peas 47
  Cream & Parmesan 48-9
  Four cheeses al forno 52
  Three cheese 49
parsley 104, 150, 158
  Butter, Parmesan, & parsley 47
  Mushroom, garlic, & parsley
    lasagne 118
  Olive oil, garlic, & parsley 129
  Parsley pesto 107
  Ricotta & herb filling, for ravioli 147
pasta machine, using 145
pasta planner chart 152-3
pasta shapes & types, pairing with
  sauces 14-19
peas 104, 150
  Butter, Parmesan, & peas 47
  Peas, prosciutto, & fresh herbs 111
  Primavera 116-17
  Primavera with cream 116
  Primavera pesto 116
Pecorino 46, 160
  Fava beans with Pecorino 123
peeling & chopping 156-9
pepper 7, 12, 151
peppers, red *see* red peppers
pesto
  Basil pesto cream 105
  Basil ricotta pesto 105
  Best basil pesto 105
  Chili olive pesto 100
  Classic genoese pesto 124
  Even simpler basil pesto 105
  Fresh tomato sauce with pesto 37
  Olive, anchovy, & caper pesto 100
  Parsley pesto 107
  Primavera pesto 116
  Red pepper pesto 138
  Red pesto 31
  Red pesto with basil 31
  Red pesto with arugula 31
  Roasted tomato with pesto 40
  Simple basil pesto 105
  Spinach & walnut pesto 106-7
  Basil pesto cream 105
  Basil ricotta pesto 105
  Best basil pesto 105
  Even simpler basil pesto 105
  Red pepper pesto 138
  Simple basil pesto 105
pine nuts 161
  Spicy eggplant with garlic, basil, &
    pine nuts 137
  Spinach, Gogonzola, & pine nut
    lasagne 118
Piquant fresh tomato 37
Piquant tuna with tomatoes 69

Pizzaiola 82-3
plain pasta, compared to egg pasta 14
porcini 56, 150, 156
  Mushroom al forno 60-1
  Porcini mushroom filling, for
    ravioli 147
  Porcini, white wine, & cream 58-9
  Tomatoes with porcini 60
potatoes, Classic genoese pesto 124
preparation techniques 156-9
Primavera 116-17
Primavera with cream 116
Primavera pesto 116
prosciutto 80
  Asparagus, prosciutto, & fresh herbs 111
  Peas, prosciutto, & fresh herbs 111
  Prosciutto & cream 81
provolone 160
  Three-cheese 49
Puttanesca 34
Puy lentils 122
  Braised Umbrian lentils 124-5

R
ragù
  Chicken, tomato, & rosemary
    ragù 92-3
  Classic Italian-American lasagne 95
  Classic lasagne al forno 94-5
  Classic ragù bolognese 91
  Ragù al forno 92
  Spicy sausage ragù 90-1
ravioli, Fresh (homemade) 146-7
Red clam sauce 74
Red mussel sauce 74-5
red onion, Fresh tomato, red onion, &
  basil 33
red peppers 134, 157
  Red pepper pesto 138
  Roasted pepper 135
  Roasted pepper & tomato sauce 140-1
  Roasted vegetables al forno 141
  Roasted vegetables with green olives
    & ricotta 138-9
red pepper flakes 150, 160
Red pesto 31
Red pesto with basil 31
Red pesto with arugula 31
reheating sauces 149
ricotta 160
  Basil ricotta pesto 105
  Classic Italian-American lasagne 95
  Eggplant, basil, & mozzarella
    lasagne 118
  Eggplant with garlic & ricotta 137
  Fresh tomato with ricotta 37
  Gorgonzola & ricotta 50
  Gorgonzola, ricotta, & baby spinach 50
  Gorgonzola, ricotta, & basil 50
  Gorgonzola, ricotta, & arugula 50
  Greens, Parmesan, & ricotta filling,
    for ravioli 147
  Mushroom, garlic, & parsley

    lasagne 118
  Ricotta & herb filling, for ravioli 147
  Roasted tomato with ricotta & basil 40
  Roasted vegetables al forno 141
  Roasted vegetables with green olives
    & ricotta 138-9
  Spinach & ricotta lasagne 118-19
  Spinach, Gogonzola, & pine nut
    lasagne 118
Roasted garlic & cherry tomatoes 130
Roasted pepper 135
Roasted tomato 40-1
Roasted tomato with crispy pancetta 40
Roasted tomato with pesto 40
Roasted tomato with ricotta & basil 40
Roasted vegetables al forno 141
Roasted vegetables with green olives &
  ricotta 138-9
rolling out fresh pasta 145
rosemary
  Chicken, tomato, & rosemary
    ragù 92-3
  Chickpeas with rosemary, chili, &
    garlic 123
  Simmered tomato with red wine &
    rosemary 42

S
saffron, Golden saffron 52
sage, Sizzling sage butter 108-9
salmon
  Salmon caviar with butter & chives 66
  Smoked salmon, vodka, & dill 64-5
  Smoked salmon with white wine,
    cream, & chives 70
salt 7, 21, 151, 161
sauces
  freezing, defrosting, & reheating 149
  pairing with pasta types &
    shapes 14-19
  tossing with pasta 25
sausages 80
  Sausage with cream & basil 84
  Spicy sausage ragù 90-1
scallions, Crispy pancetta & scallions 83
scallops
  Scallops with crème fraîche & dill 72
  Scallops with garlic & crisp crumbs 68
  Spicy garlic scallops 73
sea salt 7, 21, 151, 161
seafood
  clams
    Red clam sauce 74
    Seafood extravaganza 76-7
    White clam sauce 68
  crayfish, Seafood extravaganza 76-7
  mussels
    Red mussel sauce 74-5
    Seafood extravaganza 76-7
    White clam sauce variation 68
  salmon roe, Salmon caviar with
    butter & chives 66
  scallops

Scallops with crème fraîche & dill **72**
Scallops with garlic & crisp crumbs **68**
Spicy garlic scallops **73**
shrimp **161**
    Chili shrimp **70-1**
    Shrimp with lemon & basil **66-7**
    Seafood extravaganza **76-7**
    Spicy garlic shrimp with cherry
        tomatoes **73**
smoked salmon
    Smoked salmon, vodka, & dill **64-5**
    Smoked salmon with white wine,
        cream, & chives **70**
squid **70**
    Chili squid **70-1**
    Seafood extravaganza **76-7**
tuna **150**
    Piquant tuna with tomatoes **69**
    Tuna & tomato **69**
    Tuna with lemon & capers **64**
    see also anchovies
serving quantities
    dried pasta **20**
    fresh pasta **23**
shallots, Pan-roasted chicken with garlic
    & shallots **84-5**
short pasta **18-19, 24**
Shredded zucchini with golden
    garlic **114-15**
shrimp **161**
    Chili shrimp **70-1**
    Shrimp with lemon & basil **66-7**
    Seafood extravaganza **76-7**
    Spicy garlic shrimp with cherry
        tomatoes **73**
Sicilian eggplant with garlic **137**
Simmered tomato **42-3**
Simmered tomato with aromatics **42**
Simmered tomato with cinnamon &
    bay **42**
Simmered tomato with cream **42**
Simmered tomato with red wine &
    rosemary **42**
Simmered tomato with vodka **42**
Simple basil pesto **105**
sizes
    chopped vegetables & herbs **158-9**
    pans **7, 10-11**
Sizzling sage butter **108-9**
smoked salmon
    Smoked salmon, vodka, & dill **64-5**
    Smoked salmon with white wine,
        cream, & chives **70**
Spicy eggplant with garlic, basil, &
    pine nuts **137**
Spicy broccoli with golden garlic **112-13**
Spicy broccoli with golden garlic &
    anchovies **112**
Spicy broccoli rabe with
    golden garlic **112**
Spicy cauliflower with golden
    garlic **112**
Spicy fresh tomato sauce **37**

Spicy garlic shrimp with cherry
    tomatoes **73**
Spicy garlic scallops **73**
Spicy lemon olive **101**
Spicy sausage ragù **90-1**
spinach
    Gorgonzola, ricotta, & baby spinach **50**
    Greens, Parmesan, & ricotta filling,
        for ravioli **147**
    Spinach & ricotta lasagne **118-19**
    Spinach & walnut pesto **106-7**
    Spinach, Gogonzola, & pine nut
        lasagne **118**
    Wilted spinach with golden garlic **115**
squid **70**
    Chili squid **70-1**
    Seafood extravaganza **76-7**
steak
    Classic Italian-American lasagne **95**
    Classic lasagne al forno **94-5**
    Classic ragù bolognese **91**
    Pizzaiola **82-3**
    Ragù al forno **92**
straw & hay (paglia e fieno), cooks'
    note **66, 131**
sun-dried tomatoes **30, 161**
    Red pesto **31**
    Red pesto with basil **31**
    Red pesto with arugula **31**
    Sun-dried tomato with chili, garlic, &
        black olives **33**
swiss chard, Greens, Parmesan, &
    ricotta filling, for ravioli **147**

T

tagliatelle & tagliolini, fresh
    (homemade) **145**
tasting **7**
techniques see cooking techniques
ten commandments of cooking pasta **8**
Three cheese **49**
tomato paste **30**
tomatoes **30**
    canned tomatoes **30, 150**
        Amatriciana **86-7**
        Arrabbiata **35**
        Braised Umbrian lentils **124-5**
        Chicken, tomato, & rosemary
            ragù **92-3**
        Napolitana **35**
        Pan-cooked tomato &
            mozzarella **38-9**
        Piquant tuna with tomatoes **69**
        Pizzaiola **82-3**
        Puttanesca **34**
        Red clam sauce **74**
        Red mussel sauce **74-5**
        Roasted vegetables al forno **141**
        Simmered tomato **42-3**
        Simmered tomato with aromatics **42**
        Simmered tomato with cinnamon
            & bay **42**
        Simmered tomato with cream **42**

Simmered tomato with red wine &
    rosemary **42**
Simmered tomato with vodka **42**
Spicy sausage ragù **90-1**
Tomato & mozzarella al forno
    38-9
Tomatoes with porcini **60**
Tuna & tomato **69**
cherry tomatoes
    Shrimp with lemon & basil **66-7**
    Roasted garlic & cherry
        tomatoes **130**
    Spicy garlic shrimp with cherry
        tomatoes **73**
    Spicy garlic scallops **73**
    Tuna with lemon & capers **64**
fresh tomatoes **30, 156, 158**
    Amatriciana **86-7**
    Braised Umbrian lentils **124-5**
    Fresh tomato **32-3**
    Fresh tomato & lemon **33**
    Fresh tomato & mozzarella **33**
    Fresh tomato & olives **33**
    Fresh tomato with molten
        mozzarella **37**
    Fresh tomato, red onion, & basil **33**
    Fresh tomato with ricotta **37**
    Fresh tomato, arugula, & balsamic
        vinegar **33**
    Fresh tomato sauce **36-7**
    Fresh tomato sauce with pesto **37**
    Napolitana **35**
    Olive oil, garlic, & fresh tomato **129**
    Pan-cooked tomato &
        mozzarella **38-9**
    Piquant fresh tomato **37**
    Puttanesca **34**
    Red clam sauce **74**
    Red mussel sauce **74-5**
    Roasted pepper & tomato
        sauce **140-1**
    Roasted tomato **40-1**
    Roasted tomato with crispy
        pancetta **40**
    Roasted tomato with pesto **40**
    Roasted tomato with ricotta &
        basil **40**
    Roasted vegetables with green olives
        & ricotta **138-9**
    Spicy fresh tomato sauce **37**
    Tomato & mozzarella al forno
        38-9
sun-dried tomatoes **30, 161**
    Red pesto **31**
    Red pesto with basil **31**
    Red pesto with arugula **31**
    Sun-dried tomato with chili, garlic,
        & black olives **33**
tossing pasta with sauce **25**
tuna **150**
    Piquant tuna with tomatoes **69**
    Tuna & tomato **69**
    Tuna with lemon & capers **64**

V

Venetian-style chicken liver **88**
vodka
  Simmered tomato with vodka **42**
  Smoked salmon, vodka, & dill **64-5**

W

walnuts
  Parsley pesto **107**
  Spinach & walnut pesto **106-7**
White clam sauce **68**
wild mushrooms 56, 150, 156
  Mushroom al forno **60-1**
  Mushroom, garlic, & parsley
    lasagne **118**
  Mushroom, white wine, & cream **58-9**
  Porcini mushroom filling, for
    ravioli **147**
  Porcini, white wine, & cream **58-9**
  Tomatoes with porcini **60**
  Wild mushroom persillade **57**
Wilted leeks with golden garlic **115**
Wilted spinach with golden garlic **115**
wine 150
  Golden saffron **52**
  Mushroom, white wine, & cream **58-9**
  Pan-roasted chicken with garlic &
    shallots **84-5**
  Porcini, white wine, & cream **58-9**
  Prosciutto & cream **81**
  Simmered tomato with red wine &
    rosemary **42**
  Smoked salmon with white wine,
    cream, & chives **70**

Y

yellow peppers, Roasted vegetables with
  green olives & ricotta **138-9**
yogurt, Basil pesto cream **105**

Z

zucchini 104
  Zucchini & basil with cream **110-11**
  Zucchini with ham **111**
  Primavera **116-17**
  Primavera with cream **116**
  Primavera pesto **116**
  Shredded zucchini with golden
    garlic **114-15**

Index compiled by Sue Bosanko

MAIL ORDER SOURCES

CITARELLA
2135 Broadway
New York, NY 10023
(212)- 874-0383
www.citarella.com

Catalog available.
Specialty foods including meats, cheeses, dried
pasta, and olive oils

DEAN & DELUCA
560 Broadway
New York, NY 10021
(800)-221-7714
www.dean-deluca.com

Catalog available.
Specialty foods including Italian cheeses,
estate-bottled olive oils, lentils, dried
mushrooms, kitchen equipment.

ZABAR'S
2245 Broadway
New York, NY 10024
(800)- 697- 6301
Zabars@infohouse.com

Catalog available.
Specialty foods including Italian cheeses,
estate-bottled olive oils, caviar, smoked salmon,
dried porcini mushrooms.

SUR LA TABLE
Catalog Division
1765 Sixth Avenue South
Seattle, Washington
800-243-0852
www.surlatable.com

Catalog available.
Kitchen equipment.

HOW WE MAKE OUR BOOKS

In 1983, a tiny bookstore with a unique concept opened in London's Notting Hill. BOOKS FOR COOKS is a bookstore run by cooks for cooks, selling only cookbooks, teaching cooking classes, cooking from the books, and serving up the results in a tiny restaurant among the bookshelves.

I work in the store, cook in the kitchen, and teach in the school. It's true that I acquired my technical training as a professional chef, but to my mind, my real culinary education began the day I crossed the threshold of Books For Cooks. It's from my students and customers that I learn most about the way people live, cook, and eat today, and it's this experience that informs the way we make our books. Real food for real life is our motto. Each title is specially devised to meet the needs of today's busy cooks.

I'm lucky enough to work in a team of dedicated food lovers. We research, test, photograph, write, design, and edit our books from start to finish. All the ingredients are bought from ordinary shops and tested in a domestic kitchen. Our recipes are designed to be cooked at home. Oh yes, and it's all real food in the photographs!

You can write, phone, fax, or e-mail us any time.
We'd love to hear from you.

BOOKS FOR COOKS
4 BLENHEIM CRESCENT
LONDON W11 1NN
TEL: 020-07221-1992
FAX: 020-07221-1517

info@booksforcooks.com

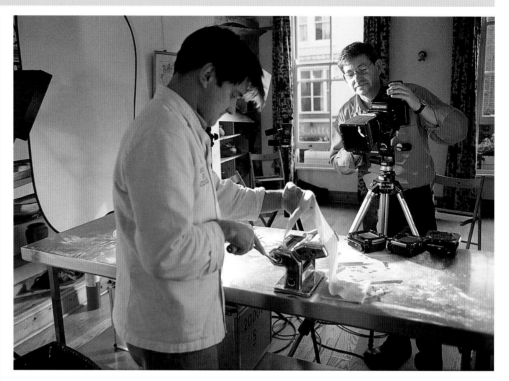